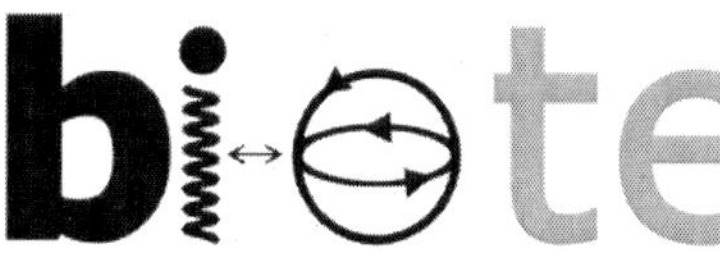

Dr. Humberto Maturana and Dr. Franciso Varela, two Chilean biologist/neuroscientists, in their ground-breaking work on Self-Organizing Living Systems chose to illustrate their core concepts with a little graphical symbol with each component having a very significant meaning:

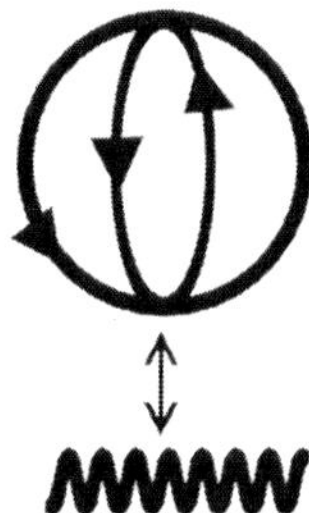

The Bioteams logo visually reminds us to always keep three very important things in mind as we design team interventions, processes, roles, behaviors, strategies, tools and enabling technologies:

1. All Bioteams are Self-Organizing Networks
2. All Bioteams have Nervous Systems
3. All Bioteams are Communications Systems

Bioteams and bioteaming are the most appropriate ways to think about teams, networks and organizations in today's interconnected world.

Also from Meghan-Kiffer Press

EXTREME COMPETITION:
INNOVATION AND THE GREAT 21ST CENTURY
BUSINESS REFORMATION

MORE FOR LESS:
THE POWER OF PROCESS MANAGEMENT

BUSINESS PROCESS MANAGEMENT:
THE THIRD WAVE

DEADLINES AND DUCT TAPE:
HOW TO MANAGE THE IT FUNCTION
FROM A BUSINESS PERSPECTIVE.

THE POWER OF PROCESS:
UNLEASHING THE SOURCE OF COMPETITIVE ADVANTAGE

IT DOESN'T MATTER:
BUSINESS PROCESSES DO

THE REAL-TIME ENTERPRISE:
COMPETING ON TIME

THE DEATH OF 'E' AND
THE BIRTH OF THE REAL NEW ECONOMY

Acclaim for our books:

Featured book recommendation
Harvard Business School's *Working Knowledge*

Book of the Year, *Internet World*

www.mkpress.com

Bioteams

How to create high performance teams and virtual groups based on nature's most successful designs

A detailed blueprint and how-to guide for building organizational teams, mobile workgroups, virtual communities and business networks that will prosper in the 21st century

Ken Thompson

Meghan-Kiffer Press
Innovation at the Intersection of Business and Technology
Tampa, Florida, USA
www.mkpress.com

Publisher's Cataloging-in-Publication Data

Thompson, Ken
Bioteams: How to create high performance teams and virtual groups based on nature's most successful designs
/ Ken Thompson – 1st ed.
p. cm.
ISBN10: 0-929652-42-8 ISBN13: 978-0-929652-42-9

1. Management 2. Technological innovation. 3. Diffusion of innovations.
4. Information technology. 5. Information Society. 6. Organizational change.
I. Thompson, Ken. II. Title

HM48.T75 2008 Library of Congress Control Number: 2007943419
303.48'33–dc22 CIP

Book's Web site: www.mkpress.com/bioteams

Published by Meghan-Kiffer Press
310 East Fern Street — Suite G
Tampa, FL 33604 USA

Meghan-Kiffer Press
USA

Printed in the United States of America. SAN 249-7980
MK Printing 10 9 8 7 6 5 4 3 2 1

To Dawn, for all her unflinching love, support and good humor in this and all my other ventures; and to my children, Scott, Nadia, Justin and Jamie for what they are constantly teaching me about the amazing power of curiosity, imagination and focus.

Barbossa: *Aye, we're good and lost now.*
Elizabeth Swann: *Lost?*
Barbossa: *For sure, you have to be lost to find a place that can't be found, elseways everyone would know where it was.*
—Captain Barbossa, Pirates of the Caribbean: At World's End, 2007

One does not discover new lands without consenting to lose sight of the shore for a very long time.
—Andre Gide, French Novelist, 1869-1951

Nature is a quarry for models which suggest solutions
—John Adair, The Art of Creative Thinking

Adapt or perish, now as ever, is nature's inexorable imperative.
—H. G. Wells (1866 - 1946)

Nature does nothing uselessly.
—Aristotle (384 BC - 322 BC)

Foreword – Dr. Curtis Bonk

To succeed in work environments today, you must be able to work in teams. In response, *Bioteams* offers a vision of what such successful teaming experiences look like in the twenty-first century. As synectics research has shown for decades, lessons and patterns from nature offer clues and insights into creative new products, procedures, and problem solving. With *Bioteams*, however, such research insightfully extends into team performances and interactions that lead to such new product inventions and effective business practices.

Ken Thompson not only lays out the research and theory, as well as an integrated set of principles related to bioteams, he backs that up with rich and insightful examples, stories, and experiences. The forms and types of bioteams covered in this book are highly intriguing and pull one into each page and chapter wanting to learn more.

Bioteams is a book about teams for teams, but it is more than that; it offers many stories, principles, and guidelines for how any individual can successfully participate in most any work or learning-related situation faced today and on into tomorrow. As such, it extends many recent management principles to the world of virtual networked business teams in which nearly everyone now participates to some degree. This book offers a chance not only to understand a wide range of interesting success stories in teaming, but outlines a set of principles and procedures to easily create your own successes.

When reading *Bioteams*, you will not solely think about the teams in which you participate, but in your role within them. To what degree are you performing as a bioteam member should, thereby, foster team creativity, innovation, and success? If you are not sure, read this book and quickly find out. If you think you know, read it anyway to find out more about how you can enhance your role.

This is the age of employee participation, multiple leaders and yet no leader, and prompt communication, as well as the technologies that make all this possible. In this intriguing book, *Bioteams*, Ken Thompson brings many separate management movements and strands together and makes sense of them. His depth and breadth of knowledge in this area is fascinating.

Curtis J. Bonk
Professor of Instructional Systems Technology, Iniana University, Author, and President of CourseShare, LLC and SurveyShare, Inc.

Foreword – Jay Cross

The biggest challenge businesses today face is unlearning what was successful in the industrial age and learning how to prosper in the network era.

Most companies are somewhere between being stuck in the past and embracing the future. Think of organizations with industrial-age beliefs as ice, because they are rigid. In addition to their orientation to control, ice organizations think business is a zero-sum game; for me to win, you must lose. They have a black-and-white view of the world; things are rigid; the fundamentals still apply. Secrecy is competition advantage; hoarding information is the norm.

Water companies are those that embrace the future. To them, reality is the unpredictable result of complex adaptive forces. Nothing's perfect; stuff happens. Cooperation is a win-win game. Relationships are all-important, and the more open you are, the easier it is to form them.

Ken Thompson has written an important book, a guidebook to help companies move from vestiges of the industrial age to the efficiencies of the network era.

Companies are not machines; they are living organisms. Yesterday's organizational teams are giving way to organic, self-organizing bioteams. Drawing on lessons from biology, ecology, and the natural world, Thompson provides wise counsel for setting up and nurturing bioteams. Here's the bottom line:

"After 3.8 billion years of research and development, failures are fossils, and what surrounds us is the secret to survival. Like the viceroy butterfly imitating the monarch, we humans are imitating the best and brightest organisms in our habitat. We are learning, for instance, how to grow food like a prairie, build ceramics like an abalone, create color like a peacock, self-medicate like a chimp, compute like a cell, and run a business like a hickory forest."

Thompson believes that today's managements misunderstand the dynamic and living nature of the team as an entity over and above its membership. The natural attributes of bioteams include:

- *Collective Leadership.* Any group member can take the lead.
- *Instant Messaging.* Instant, whole-group, broadcast communications.
- *Ecosystems.* Small is Beautiful … but Big is Powerful.
- *Clustering.* Engaging many through the few.

Thompson provides a prescription for managing bioteams naturally. Most of his advice applies equally well to the enterprise the bioteams collectively support. For example, managers should communicate information, not orders: "Give me the dots but let me connect them for myself." It's the team's job to find and process new information.

You plant a seed and expect nature to do the rest. Give workers the resources and challenge them to do what's required. Rather than give them an extra push, enable them to achieve accountability through transparency, not permission.

Thompson wants to define the team in terms of "network transformations" – not outputs. I think of this as "Trust the force, Luke." As Henry Ford once said, "If a man thinks he can do something or that he can't, he's right."

The conclusions about bioteams are bolstered with examples from high performing banks, manufacturers, sports, and more. Thompson highlights the future norms of doing business: transparency, trust the team, shared glory, incremental improvement, and clear accountability.

The core messages of *Bioteams* provide a guide to the managerial future. We are all leaders. We must keep one another informed in real time. We trust living systems to self-organize.

Thompson describes the best practices of business in the network era. Read this book if you want to know what's going on. Ironically, these are not really Thompson's rules; they are Mother Nature's.

Jay Cross
CEO, Internet Time Group, LLC, and author of
Informal Learning and *Implementing E-Learning*

Preface

This is not a biology book. It is a book about using lessons from biology to improve the workings of mobile and virtual teams, groups, networks and communities. This is an area where I have been working extensively as a leader and a coach for the last 20 years. The book is the product of three years study and synthesis of the work of many of the leading scientists in various biological and ecological disciplines. These include established luminaries such as Edward O. Wilson, Lynn Margulis, Humberto Maturana, Fritjof Capra, Craig Reynolds, Arie De Geus and Howard Rheingold. In addition, I have also drawn on the work of more recent pioneers such as Robert Axelrod, Albert Barabasi, Carl Andersen and Raul Espejo. Some of the esteemed individuals were generous enough to offer personal answers to my many questions. All mistakes and misinterpretations are, of course, totally my own responsibility.

The basic bioteams theory was pretty much complete by mid-2006 and I was able to use my blog (www.bioteams.com) to test and refine the key ideas with the broad community of collaboration practitioners. These folks were never shy to comment about what they liked, disliked or felt was unclear or ambiguous. These practitioners have my grateful thanks – too many to mention but they know who they are!

I decided not to publish anything in book form at this stage as I wanted time for myself and others to test out the bioteams ideas in practice to see well how they held up and where they needed to be refined. Nobody needs another book of new but untried management theories about teams! Over the last 18 months the various bioteaming principles have been tried, tested and refined with actual teams, some of which are described in detail in the case studies section of the book. What you read here reflects and incorporates this experience – a new theory for team and group performance improvement that has been tested in practice with real teams!

I would also like to thank Robin Good, whose excellent skills of articulation helped me sharpen and clarify the core concepts as we worked together on the original articles and manifesto that started it all.

Ken Thompson
Belfast, Northern Ireland

Summary Contents

FOREWORD – DR. CURTIS BONK 6

FOREWORD – JAY CROSS 7

PREFACE 9

PART 1: BIOTEAMS INTRODUCED 21

1. BIOTEAMS AND BIOMIMICRY 21

2. ORGANIZATIONAL TEAMS JUST BECAME EXTINCT 23

3. WHAT NATURE TEACHES US ABOUT TEAMS 31

4. HOW CAN WE DO BETTER THAN NATURE'S TEAMS? 35

5. AN OVERVIEW OF BIOTEAMING 38

6. BIRDS DO IT AND GREAT TEAMS DO IT, TOO 44

7. THE STATE OF BIOTEAMING 55

PART 2: BIOTEAMING – THE DETAILED MODEL 57

8. HIDDEN BELIEFS OF HIGH PERFORMING TEAMS 57

9. THE BIOTEAMS LEADERSHIP ZONE 63

10. THE BIOTEAMS CONNECTIVITY ZONE 69

11. THE BIOTEAMS EXECUTION ZONE 78

12. THE BIOTEAMS ORGANIZATION ZONE 88

PART 3: THE MECHANISMS OF BIOTEAMING 101

13. PHEROMONE-STYLE COMMUNICATIONS 101

14. FOUR UNIQUE WAYS BIOTEAMS GET THINGS DONE 107

15. THE SIX KEY PROCESSES IN A BIOTEAM 110

16. THREE COMMUNICATION PATTERNS IN BIOTEAMS 114

17. THE 4 TYPES OF TEAMWORK IN A BIOTEAM 116

18. THE THREE TYPES OF RECOGNITION IN BIOTEAMS 120

19. THE THREE RINGS OF COMMITMENT IN A BIOTEAM 122

20. USING "LIVING SYSTEMS THEORY" 124
21. "REQUISITE VARIETY" IN BIOTEAMS 129
22. ECOSYSTEMS AND BIOTEAMS 132

PART 4: MEASURING BIOTEAM SUCCESS 135
23. A TEAM PERFORMANCE IMPROVEMENT SCORECARD 135

PART 5: SEVEN KEY BIOTEAMING TECHNIQUES 142
24. INTRODUCTION TO THE BIOTEAM TECHNIQUES 142

PART 6: BIOTEAMING CASE STUDIES 161
25. OVERVIEW OF CASE STUDIES 161

PART 7: FUTURE DIRECTIONS IN BIOTEAMS 201
26. BIOCROWDS – THE NEXT EVOLUTION 201

INDEX – NOT 206
REFERENCES 206
ABOUT THE AUTHOR 210

Extensive Contents

To better serve as a reference aid, we have included an extensive table of contents instead of an index.

FOREWORD – DR. CURTIS BONK 6

FOREWORD – JAY CROSS 7

PREFACE 9

PART 1: BIOTEAMS INTRODUCED 21

1. BIOTEAMS AND BIOMIMICRY 21
   - Biomimicry is about learning from nature 21
   - Bioteaming is biomimetics for group behavior 22

2. ORGANIZATIONAL TEAMS JUST BECAME EXTINCT 23
   - Organizational Teams are not delivering 23
   - Organizational Teams are using the wrong model 23
   - Organizational teams are no longer fit for their environments 25
   - The challenges facing Virtual Networked Business Teams 26
   - Statistics on Virtual Networked Teams 27
   - Are Internet Technologies a solution to these problems? 28
   - The Bioteaming Breakthrough 29

3. WHAT NATURE TEACHES US ABOUT TEAMS 31
   - Bioteaming Introduced 31
   - Key Characteristics of Nature's Teams 31
   - Collective Leadership 31
   - Instant Messaging 32
   - Ecosystems 32
   - Clustering 33

4. HOW CAN WE DO BETTER THAN NATURE'S TEAMS? 35
   - Intelligence and Autonomy 35
   - The impact of individual team beliefs on overall performance 36
   - Uncovering the "hidden beliefs" of high performing teams 36

5. AN OVERVIEW OF BIOTEAMING 38
   - Bioteams Leadership Zone 39
   - Bioteams Connectivity Zone 40
   - Bioteams Execution Zone 40
   - Bioteams Organization Zone 42

6. BIRDS DO IT AND GREAT TEAMS DO IT, TOO 44
   - GREAT ENTERPRISES DO IT 44
     - Capital One Bank 44

Schlumberger 45
General Electric 45
Southwest Airlines 46
GREAT ORGANIZATIONS DO IT 46
Humberside Training and Enterprise Council (TEC) 46
9-11 Crisis Response Team 47
GREAT NETWORKS AND SUPPLY CHAINS DO IT 48
Boeing 48
The film industry 49
GREAT CAUSES DO IT 50
Open Source Software 50
Smart Mobs 50
GREAT SPORTS TEAMS DO IT 51
The Boston Red Sox 51
Great Soccer Teams 52
Northern Ireland's Soccer Team 53
Olympic Rowing Crews 54

7. THE STATE OF BIOTEAMING 55
Dr. R. Meredith Belbin 55
Global Interest in Bioteaming 56

PART 2: BIOTEAMING – THE DETAILED MODEL 57

8. HIDDEN BELIEFS OF HIGH PERFORMING TEAMS 57
Belief 1. Clear and Public Accountability 57
Belief 2. Trusted Competency 57
Belief 3. Give and Take 57
Belief 4. Total Transparency 58
Belief 5. Shared Glory 58
Belief 6. Meaningful Mission Value 58
Belief 7. Outcome Optimism 59
Good beliefs make a team work harder 59
Bioteaming includes identifying your team's beliefs 59
HIGH PERFORMING TEAMS BELIEFS RESEARCH 59
Background and Context 59
Summary of the research results 60
Conclusions we drew from these results 61

9. THE BIOTEAMS LEADERSHIP ZONE 63
LEADERSHIP ZONE: RULE 1 - SEND OUT TIMELY INFORMATION 63
It's all about spotting Opportunities and Threats 63
But why don't nature's teams issue orders? 63
One-way is okay 64
Roger and Wilco 65

LEADERSHIP ZONE: RULE 2 - EVERYONE MUST BROADCAST 66
The Queen is Blind 66
Team Vital Signs 66
LEADERSHIP ZONE: RULE 3 – ACT, DON'T ASK (PERMISSION GRANTED) 67
Permission Structures 67
Team Transparency 68
The Importance of Reputation Systems 68

10. THE BIOTEAMS CONNECTIVITY ZONE 69
CONNECTIVITY ZONE: RULE 4 - ALWAYS ON/ALWAYS NEAR 69
Survival of the Fastest 69
Organizational teams don't operate Hot-Lines 70
So how can we exploit the Bioteam Hotline? 70
Benefits of "Always On/Always Near" 71
CONNECTIVITY ZONE: RULE 5 – OUT-TEAM 71
Nature collaborates to compete 71
What is Symbiogenesis? 72
Principles of Symbiogenesis 72
Why does nature love symbiosis? 73
So what would a bioteam do? 74
Benefits of "Out-Teaming" 74
CONNECTIVITY ZONE: RULE 6 - NURTURE THE NETWORK 75
The power of weak ties 76
Good teams need both strong and weak ties 76

11. THE BIOTEAMS EXECUTION ZONE 78
EXECUTION ZONE: RULE 7 – SWARM! 78
Nature's Way 78
"Boids" 78
Benefits of Rule to Nature 79
Application of Rule to Organizational Teams 79
O-R-G-A-N-I-C team member behaviors 80
3-Dimensional Team Members 80
Benefits of Rule to Organizational Teams 80
EXECUTION ZONE: RULE 8 – TIT FOR TAT 80
Nature's Way 81
Sticklebacks play TIT FOR TAT 81
Some weaknesses in TFT 81
Benefits of Rule to Nature 82
Application of Rule to Organizational Teams 82
Win-Win is a state, not a strategy 83
Benefits of Rule to Organizational Teams 83
EXECUTION ZONE: RULE 9 – TEAM-BASED GENETIC ALGORITHM ... 84

Nature's Way.....84
But normal evolution is too slow.....84
Songbirds – an example of accelerated evolution.....85
Benefits of Rule to Nature.....85
Application of Rule to Organizational Teams.....85
Implementing Team-based Genetic Algorithms.....85

12. THE BIOTEAMS ORGANIZATION ZONE.....88

ORGANIZATION ZONE: RULE 10 – AUTOPOIESIS (SELF-ORGANIZATION).....88
Nature's Way.....88
1. The Self-Organizing Network.....89
2. The Nervous System.....89
3. The Communications System.....89
Benefits of Rule to Nature.....90
Application of Rule to Organizational Teams.....90
Benefits of Rule to Organizational Teams.....92

ORGANIZATION ZONE: RULE 11 – POROUS MEMBRANES.....92
Nature's Way.....92
Benefits of Rule to Nature.....93
Application of Rule to Organizational Teams.....93
Good stuff gets in.....93
Bad stuff stays out.....93
Benefits of Rule to Organizational Teams.....95

ORGANIZATION ZONE: RULE 12 – EMERGE!.....95
Nature's Way.....95
The Founding Stage.....96
The Ergonomic Stage.....96
The Reproductive Stage.....97
The Terminal Stage (i.e., Death!).....97
Benefits of Rule to Nature.....97
Application of Rule to Organizational Teams.....98
The Founding Stage.....98
The Ergonomic Stage.....98
The Reproductive Stage.....99
The Terminal Stage (i.e., Death!).....99
Benefits of Rule to Organizational Teams.....99

PART 3: THE MECHANISMS OF BIOTEAMING.....101

13. PHEROMONE-STYLE COMMUNICATIONS.....101
Introduction to Pheromone Signaling.....101
13 Characteristics of Pheromone Signaling.....102
1. Broadcast and Individual:.....102

2. 1-way: 102
3. Whole species: 102
4. Simple vocabulary: 103
5. Intraspecies and Interspecies: 103
6. Robust Delivery: 103
7. Low energy: 104
8. Longevity potential: 104
9. Message Range: 104
10. Multichannel: 105
11. Quick and Slow Responses: 105
12. Anonymity of sender: 105
13. Location Information: 105

14. FOUR UNIQUE WAYS BIOTEAMS GET THINGS DONE 107

Four habits of bioteams 107
1. One knows – all know! 107
2. Ask the network 107
3. Co-invention 107
4. Leveraged Engagement 109

15. THE SIX KEY PROCESSES IN A BIOTEAM 110

Natural Team Processes 110
A bioteam is a self-organizing network 110
Process 1. Foraging 111
Process 2. Co-Evolution 111
Process 3. Reproduction 112
Process 4. Nurture 112
Process 5. Maintenance 112
Process 6. Metabolism 113
Bioteam processes interlock 113

16. THREE COMMUNICATION PATTERNS IN BIOTEAMS 114

Nature's Team communication patterns 114
Shouting 114
Whispering 114
Gossiping 115

17. THE 4 TYPES OF TEAMWORK IN A BIOTEAM 116

What is "Teamwork?" 116
A Biological definition of "teamwork" 116
Teams undertake different kinds of tasks 116
Individual Tasks 116
Group Tasks 117
Partitioned Tasks 117

Team Tasks ... 117
What blend of "teamwork" is your team? ... 118
You need all flavors of teamwork in your team. ... 118

18. THE THREE TYPES OF RECOGNITION IN BIOTEAMS ... 120

Three types of recognition in nature ... 120
Species Recognition ... 120
Kin Recognition ... 120
Individual Recognition ... 121

19. THE THREE RINGS OF COMMITMENT IN A BIOTEAM .. 122

One ring to rule them – one ring to bind them! ... 122
The Three Rings ... 122
The Inner Ring ... 122
The Middle Ring ... 122
The Outer Ring ... 122
Using the three rings ... 122
You need all three rings! ... 123

20. USING "LIVING SYSTEMS THEORY" ... 124

Autopoiesis is the word! ... 124
The Four components of a living system ... 125
1. *The Boundary:* ... 125
2. *The Processes:* ... 125
3. *The Nervous System:* ... 125
4. *The Communication Channels:* ... 125
The three nested levels of system within a team or group ... 125
Applying living systems concepts to social systems ... 127
So, are your teams growing or dying? ... 128

21. "REQUISITE VARIETY" IN BIOTEAMS ... 129

How do teams optimize for their environment? ... 129
How does nature achieve Requisite Variety? ... 130
How can a human team achieve Requisite Variety? ... 130
Amplification and Attenuation ... 131

22. ECOSYSTEMS AND BIOTEAMS ... 132

Three Key Ecosystem Concepts ... 132
Community Assembly ... 132
Food Web Relationships ... 132
Complex interdependencies and feedback loops ... 133

PART 4: MEASURING BIOTEAM SUCCESS ... 135

23. A TEAM PERFORMANCE IMPROVEMENT SCORECARD ... 135

Realization of Bioteam's Benefits....135
Direct Results versus Benefits....135
The Overall Bioteam's Measurement Process in Context....135
The Bioteam's model scorecard – Leadership Zone....136
The Bioteam's model scorecard – Connectivity Zone....137
The Bioteam's model scorecard – Execution Zone....138
The Bioteam's model scorecard – Organization Zone....139
Summary Scorecard....140
Leadership Zone....140
Connectivity Zone....141

PART 5: SEVEN KEY BIOTEAMING TECHNIQUES....142

24. INTRODUCTION TO THE BIOTEAM TECHNIQUES....142
Why, what, who, how and when?....142
There is no standard bioteams roadmap....143
TECHNIQUE T1: SYMBIOSIS....143
Symbiosis....143
Purpose....143
Objectives....143
Background....144
How to use it....144
TECHNIQUE T2: PREDATOR-PARASITE (PP)....146
Predator-Parasite....146
Purpose....146
Background....146
Objectives....147
How to use it....147
TECHNIQUE T3: TEAM METABOLISM....150
Metabolism....150
Purpose....150
Objectives....150
Background....150
How to use it....150
TECHNIQUE T4: SWARMING....152
Swarming....152
Purpose....152
Objectives....152
Background....152
How to use it....153
O-R-G-A-N-I-C team member behaviors....153
Develop the Team Stimulus-Response Code....154
TECHNIQUE T5: TIT FOR TAT (TFT)....154
Tit for Tat....154

Purpose 154
Objectives 155
Background 155
How to use it 155
Win-Win is a state, not a strategy 156
TECHNIQUE T6: TEAM TIES 156
Team Ties 156
Purpose 156
Objectives: 157
Background 157
Effective teams have good internal and external networks 157
The importance of strong ties in teams 157
The importance of weak ties in teams 158
How to use it 158
TECHNIQUE T7: CELL DIVISION 159
Cell Division 159
Purpose 159
Objectives 160
Background 160
How to use it 160

PART 6: BIOTEAMING CASE STUDIES 161

25. OVERVIEW OF CASE STUDIES 161
ETC: VIRTUAL ENTERPRISE NETWORK 162
1. The Bioteam 162
2. Background and Context 162
3. Objectives 163
4. How bioteaming was used 163
5. Results Achieved 168
6. Lessons Learned: 169
7. Team Member Feedback 169
DAISYHILL: HOSPITAL INTERMEDIATE CARE TEAM 170
1. The Bioteam 170
2. Background and Context 170
3. Objectives 171
4. How bioteaming was used 172
5. Results Achieved 173
6. Lessons Learned 173
7. Team Member Feedback 174
CTSL: TELECOMS INDUSTRY WORKING PARTY 175
1. The Bioteam 175
2. Background and Context 175
3. Objectives 176

4. How bioteaming was used 177
5. Results Achieved 180
6. Lessons Learned 181
7. Team Member Feedback 182
8. Sample Terms of Reference for a Bioteam Work Group 182
DK: CONFERENCE ORGANIZATION 185
1. The Bioteam 185
2. Background and Context 185
3. Objectives 186
4. How bioteaming was used 186
5. Results Achieved 188
7. Team Member Feedback 189
LANCELOT: VIRTUAL LANGUAGE SCHOOL 190
1. The Bioteam 190
2. Background and Context 190
3. Objectives 191
4. How bioteaming was used 191
5. Results Achieved 193
6. Lessons Learned 194
7. Team Member Feedback 195
KHARMA45: MUSIC FAN ENGAGEMENT 196
1. The Bioteam 196
2. Background and Context 196
3. Objectives 197
4. How bioteaming was used 197
5. Results Achieved 199
6. Lessons Learned 200
7. Team Member Feedback 200

PART 7: FUTURE DIRECTIONS IN BIOTEAMS 201

26. BIOCROWDS – THE NEXT EVOLUTION 201

Mass Collaboration and Virtual Crowds 201
What can nature's large-scale teams teach us about Internet-based Mass Collaboration? 202
Give and Take 202
Needles in Haystacks 203
Participation through Passion 204

INDEX – NOT 206

REFERENCES 206

ABOUT THE AUTHOR 210

Part 1: Bioteams Introduced

1. Bioteams and biomimicry

Go to the ant, thou sluggard; consider her ways, and be wise.
—Proverbs 6:6

Biomimicry is about learning from nature

Learning from mother nature's designs has now officially entered the scientific mainstream. The new scientific discipline, biomimicry (also known as *biomimetics*), is gaining a lot of attention. Biomimicry is defined as "taking ideas from nature and implementing them in technologies such as engineering, design, computing, etc." Bryony Schwan, Executive Director of the Biomimicry Institute, elaborates, "Biomimicry (from bios, meaning life, and mimesis, meaning to imitate) is a new science that studies nature's best ideas and then imitates these designs and processes to solve human problems. Studying a leaf to invent a better solar cell is an example of this "innovation inspired by nature."

"The core idea is that nature, imaginative by necessity, has already solved many of the problems we are grappling with. Animals, plants, and microbes are the consummate engineers. They have found what works, what is appropriate, and most important, what lasts here on Earth. This is the real news of biomimicry: After [nature's] 3.8 billion years of research and development, failures are fossils, and what surrounds us is the secret to survival. Like the viceroy butterfly imitating the monarch, we humans are imitating the best and brightest organisms in our habitat. We are learning, for instance, how to grow food like a prairie, build ceramics like an abalone, create color like a peacock, self-medicate like a chimp, compute like a cell, and run a business like a hickory forest."

As reported in *The Economist: Technology Quarterly,* June 2005, "The concept is very old – the Chinese wanted to make artificial silk 3,000 years ago; Daedalus' wings were one of biomimetics' early design failures. In fields from robot design to materials science, engineers are increasingly borrowing mechanisms from nature – an approach known as biomimetics. Nature's designs are, after all, the results of millions of years of trial and error."

Modern day biomimetrics really began in the 1940's when a Swiss inventor noticed how particular plant seeds attached themselves to his clothes. Under closer examination he observed this was due to a unique "hook and loop" system that led to him inventing our much loved "Velcro." Interest in biomimetics has taken until very recently to gather significant momentum because only now can our science base really cope with the advanced techniques and technologies required to exploit biomimetics.

Wikipedia serves up some additional examples, "One example is the attempt to learn from, and emulate the incredible ability of, termites to maintain virtually constant temperature and humidity in their Sub-Saharan Africa homes, despite an outside temperature variation from 3 °C and 42 °C (35 °F at night to 104 °F during the day.) Project TERMES (Termite Emulation of Regulatory Mound Environments by Simulation) scanned a termite mound, created 3-D images of the mound structure and provided the first ever glimpse of construction that may likely change the way we build our own buildings. The Eastgate Centre, a mid-rise office complex in Harare, Zimbabwe, (highlighted in a Biomimicry Institute case-study) stays cool without air conditioning and uses only 10% of the energy of a conventional building its size.

"Another example of biomimicry is modeling the echolocation of bats in darkness and adapting that functionality into a cane for the visually impaired. Research performed at the University of Leeds (in the U.K.) led to the UltraCane, a product manufactured, marketed and sold by Sound Foresight Ltd."

Bioteaming is biomimetics for group behavior

The main focus of biomimetics (or biomimicry) is engineering and learning from individual living systems. However, I strongly believe that an equally profitable focus will be to help us learn from nature's groups as well as its individuals and looking at how they cooperate as well as how they are engineered. But before we look further into "bioteams" we need to ask ourselves: "What is the problem for which a bioteam is the solution?" *The problem is that today's Organizational Teams don't work.*

2. Organizational Teams just became extinct

Organizational Teams are not delivering

Over the last ten years organizational teams have become more distributed and very complex. Despite the number of technologies available to assist teams and groups, it is still exceedingly difficult to manage teams.

I use the term 'organizational' very loosely. By "organizational teams," I mean teams working within organizations that could be solid, vertically integrated corporate entities, government departments, networked business clusters, 'not for profit' communities, informal "task forces," social grouping and special interest groups.

Individual team members may belong to many of these teams on a part-time and ad hoc basis – they may see each other frequently, or never ever meet physically – conducting all communications electronically or via the web.

And contrary to popular belief, the introduction of new real-time conferencing and collaboration technologies can actually make things worse. It may distract team members from their real business objectives and drive them into ongoing loops of technology experimentation. In these situations, the focus on the work mission is often lost in favor of mastering and attempting to extract ever increasing benefits from the technology itself.

So why is it so difficult to successfully manage teams today?

I believe there are two main reasons:

- Teams are using the wrong model to organize themselves
- Teams are not keeping pace with the rapid changes in their business environments

Organizational Teams are using the wrong model

The underlying model in almost all teams today is "command and control." In simple terms, this means that the members of the team wait for instructions issued by their single team leader. These leaders have limited span of control, so if the team grows beyond a certain size they will create a management structure to help them lead. The team members report back as they complete their tasks and they are given new ones. They also escalate "upward" any issues and problems that they can't resolve themselves and await guidance from the leader on what to do next.

These teams can have huge amount of member "down-time" where one piece of work is completed but instructions are needed on the next task. Or, a problem has cropped up that has been pushed up through the "chain of command" to the leader for guidance before work can continue. In a team like, this it is nearly always safer for a team member to do nothing if faced by a new problem than to take initiative.

You can think of two extremes of team 'work style' as shown below:

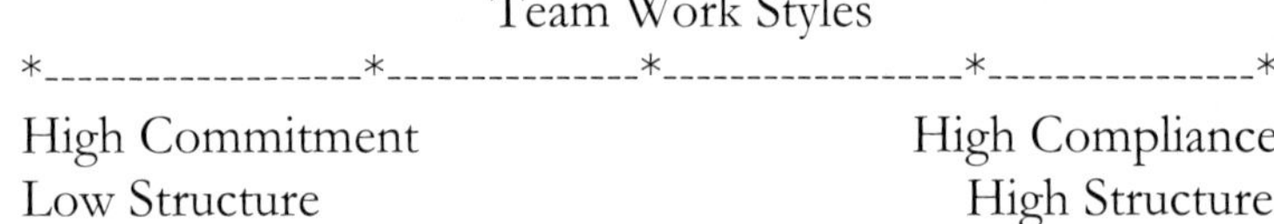

On the far left we have a high commitment team but with very little structure, an extreme example might be a family on holiday fleeing from a rampaging elephant.

On the extreme right we have a totally compliant team with lots of structure but little commitment, an example might be prisoners doing heavy labor on work detail.

The current 'command and control' model places Organizational teams well over on the right side of the spectrum, high on compliance but low on commitment.

It seems obvious that a better model would place Organizational Teams nearer to the center of the picture, the optimum balance of commitment (passion) and compliance (structure).

But surely today's enlightened managers are no longer using such an out-of-date model to manage their teams?

Facts show otherwise – the single leader command and control team is very much alive and well in our business, government, not for profit and social sectors. You only have to watch the popularity of programs such as "The Apprentice," which showcases Alan Sugar's authoritarian style of "hire and fire" management.

Command and control is totally the wrong model for today's teams. Command and control was invented by the military and was adopted by organizations. It was a great model for mass warfare where you needed to be sure your team would instantly do what they had to do. This worked well because the job at hand was often something a team member would never do naturally, like climbing out of a safe trench into harm's way. It was also a great model for mass production where you needed above all to ensure consistency of action in team members.

Today's teams need a model that gives them some enabling structure but not at the expense of destroying their autonomy and initiative. This is definitely not command and control. I propose a new model, "bioteaming," that I will explain fully in the coming sections.

Organizational teams are no longer fit for their environments

Nowadays, it is rare to find teams in which individuals all know each other, sit in the same work area each day, work the same hours, share common physical work spaces, belong to and are paid by the same organization, have a common business culture and enjoy some degree of prior history of working together.

Today's teams are a complex alliance of individuals from different organizations, departments, professions, and locations. Each member has a different skill set and is accustomed to using different technology tools. Today's teams are comprised of individuals with different backgrounds, languages, cultures and education and involved in team activities in broadly varying degrees.

Today's teams are a very different animal compared to those many of us grew up with. In fact, the differences between past teams and today's are so significant that a new name is needed for today's teams, I like to refer to them as *Virtual Networked Teams.*

"Virtual" means that the team is dependent on Internet technologies more so than before. Less obvious, but equally significant, is the fact that "virtual" also means that the team operates with "virtual capacity." Here virtual means "not physically present." This also means that the team can constantly grow and shrink according to its needs.

"Networked" means that the team is made of dispersed and physically distant individuals who are interconnected and operate as an organic entity. These individuals do not utilize traditional reporting hierarchies; thus "command and control" approaches are totally ineffective.

We, therefore, define a Virtual Networked Business Team as a team created by bringing together one or more cooperating groups of people to achieve a business objective. Such objectives could include:

- Designing and developing open-source software.
- Planning and launching a major event.
- Market testing of a new product with consumers.
- Defining a marketing awareness or advertising campaign.
- Implementing improved business processes.
- Planning and executing a change management and training initiatives.
- Developing and mobilizing a set of supporters for a good cause.
- Engaging, growing and energizing a fan base, like that of music or sports fans.
- Developing brand awareness in partnership with a network of "brand ambassadors."

We know that in the near future Virtual Networked Business Teams will be the dominant means for getting major work done.

The challenges facing Virtual Networked Business Teams

Is it more difficult to operate a Virtual Networked Business Team than a traditional team? I believe the answer is a resounding YES for four main reasons:

1. *The Virtual Factor*: The "Virtual factor" is the first tangible obstacle that can be felt when dealing with the optimization of a virtual networked team. The challenge in successfully engaging a team in which many of the members have never met face –to-face can be quite surprising. Members of a virtual team may never attend a physical meeting with their colleagues. Their accessibility and communication modes may vary from one team member to the next.
2. *The Network Factor*: A Networked team does not share common reporting lines, business cultures and professional sensibilities. This makes it difficult to agree on standards, accountability structures and sanctions for non-performance.

3. *The Technology Factor*: Technology is often a team component with its own cost of adoption and integration. The technology price to be paid by virtual networked teams can be daunting. Teams are often scared, if not altogether resistant, to the addition of new technologies that require steep learning curves and the adoption of unintuitive workflows. New technologies can be seen as an intrusive partner that demands a lot but doesn't actually accomplish anything. They can be obstacles to getting the "real work" done; this is particularly true in the early stages of team formation.
4. *The Business Factor*: In addition to the virtual, network and technology factors, work pressure driven by today's work environments creates the perfect recipe for stress. This stress will show itself in work groups by replacing harmonious and pro-active group support with destructive behaviors such as hiding from responsibilities, free-riding and tattle-telling.

Statistics on Virtual Networked Teams

Virtual Networked Teams are a relatively young phenomenon. There is little hard evidence available for how well they perform in real-world scenarios. However, one of the earliest forms of a Virtual Networked Team is the typical IT project team.

By its very nature the IT team is cross-functional and heavily interconnected (Networked). It integrates a wide mix of specialists (e.g., IT, change management and business staff). IT teams also embody some of the virtual factor as they expand and shrink (via the hiring of short-term consultants) according to the amount and complexity of assigned projects.

Statistics on IT project teams provide some enlightening information:

- Only a third of change initiatives achieve their objectives (OPP Survey May 2004)
- 74% of IT projects are unsuccessful (Standish Group Report 2000)
- Only 1 in 5 IT projects are likely to bring full satisfaction to their organizational sponsors (OASIG Study 1995)

These numbers reveal the quantifiable evidence that there is something deeply wrong in the way Virtual Networked Teams are operating in today's organizations.

Are Internet Technologies a solution to these problems?

With the emergence and maturing of a vast array of corporate-strength intranets, extranets, portals, Web2.0 and its multitude of supporting real-time and asynchronous communications tools, there would appear to be a huge potential for technology to bring real gains to team productivity.

This would seem to be particularly true for those teams that are physically distributed or that are highly mobile. Few people would dispute the potential benefits of effective real-time communication tools or of shared and secure workspaces. However, in practical terms, hardly any of the supposed benefits are generally realized by teams utilizing these technologies.

Why is that?

Typically, teams trying to be more effective through technology run into serious problems in trying to make it work for them, including:

- *Technology adoption*: the investment needed to learn the technology greatly exceeds the potential benefits.
- *Accountability issues*: teams find it much easier to break virtual commitments than verbal ones.
- *Team mobilization*: technology per se does not generally address the need for mobilizing action. It leaves teams using new tools without having first asked the proper strategic questions: who am I, where am I going, why do I want to get there?
- *New Working Practices*: novel and unfamiliar working practices are just too difficult to adopt within a short amount of time
- *Over focus on Technology and Process*: not enough focus on production of results

I believe that Internet Technologies are as much a part of the problem as they are a part of the solution. Though they may be very useful, they are not the critical determinant that will determine how effectively any group of networked individuals will cooperate toward the achievement of a business goal.

So what is MISSING?

The Bioteaming Breakthrough

The fundamental thing missing from teams today is the recognition of the dynamic and living nature of the team itself as a separate and distinct entity from that of its individual members.

A team is a living entity in and of itself – more than the sum of its members' abilities. For example, an ant colony, one of nature's most efficient and successful living teams, has a life of its own – albeit intimately connected to the lives of its members.

However, in organizations we treat our teams mechanistically. We think of our teams more like clocks or engines that are assigned to specific tasks and assignments. We want the highest control of them, and we want them to be very predictable in their work behavior. That's exactly the opposite of what nature's teams do. Interpretation of the team as a whole, living entity, allows a more insightful interpretation of the most efficient courses of team action.

The team is in itself a "super-organism," and as such it needs to be treated in ways that enhance and support its complex and interconnected nature. If you can see the team as a whole, and not as the mere aggregation of the individual parts that make it up, you can discover how much more productive, reliable and efficient a virtual team can be.

Once you wrap your mind around this new way of looking at organizational teams, you immediately need to rethink how such teams should be nurtured, organized and supported in effective and suitable ways.

This is why I am proposing in this book that we look at nature's most successful biological teams to uncover the secrets of extended cooperation and effective collaboration.

Nature offers us such an invaluable heritage of "best lessons learned" for how teams should be run and is the foundation for the new discipline I call "bioteaming."

Nature-derived lessons have been tested and tried over the course of hundreds of thousands of years under an infinite number of variables and scenarios. The approaches that did not work are long gone. The fact of evolution means that the study of nature's teams is the study of only the best of nature's teams.

If we are smart enough to humbly analyze and dissect the core characterizing traits of nature's successful team behaviors, we can devise and architect their use and growth within our human-based teams.

This is the mission of Bioteaming: a painstaking review and application of the common traits of nature's most effective biological teams so that we can transfer the learning to our organizational teams.

3. What nature teaches us about teams

Bioteaming Introduced

Bioteaming is about building organizational teams that operate on the basis of the natural principles that underpin nature's most successful teams. Nature's most effective bioteams include:

- Single-celled and multicellular organisms
- The human immune system and nervous system (including the brain)
- Micro-organisms such as bacteria and social insects (ants, bees and termites)
- Jellyfish, geese, monkeys, dolphins, big cats
- Forests, rivers, ecosystems, the earth (as Gaia)

Key Characteristics of Nature's Teams

My research has identified a small number of characteristics of nature's teams that are not usually present in organizational teams:

1. *Collective Leadership.* Any group member can take the lead.
2. *Instant Messaging.* Instant whole-group broadcast communications.
3. *Ecosystems.* Small is Beautiful … but Big is Powerful.
4. *Clustering.* Engaging many through the few.

Collective Leadership

Any group member can take the lead.

Nature's groups are never led exclusively by one member; different group members lead as needed.

When geese migrate it is well known that the goose leading the V formation rotates. However, this is not just because they get tired and need to fly in another goose's slipstream for a while. The real reason is that no one goose knows the whole migration route. Collectively, between them, they know the migration route but no one individual knows.

So a goose leads the part of the journey where it knows the way and when it recognizes "I don't know where to go next" it flies back into the V and waits for another goose to take over.

I call this "Collective Leadership," the right leader for the right task at the right time.

The human species seems to be the only species that trusts in a single leader (or small management team) to know the whole path, on behalf of the community.

Multi-Leader groups possess much greater agility, initiative and resilience than groups that are only led by a single exclusive leader.

Instant Messaging

Instant whole-group broadcast communications.

Nature's groups use short instant messages that are instantly broadcast and received "in situ" wherever the receivers are. These messages are very short and very simple – essentially just two types:

- *Opportunity Messages.* Food, nesting materials, Prey
- *Threat Messages.* Predators, Rival colonies

Ants achieve such messaging by using a range of chemical pheromones that they emit and lay in trails, and that are instantly picked up by the other ants. Bees use dances, for example, the waggle dance that is danced by a hive member who has found a food supply. The hive mates watch the dance and the angle of the axis of the dance points them to the food supply. It is important to note that:

- These messages are group broadcasts and are not replied to.
- They are received and acted upon immediately; there is no concept of a 2-stage communication that is received at point A and acted on later at point B.

A critical point is that these instant messages are so simple they really act just as "alerts." The recipient has to "decide" what to do. Such instant messages do not convey orders or instructions.

Ecosystems

Small is Beautiful .....but Big is Powerful.

In nature, the size of the group is always right for the job and small groups link into bigger groups, that in turn link into still bigger groups.

In the chapter, "The four types of teamwork in a bioteam," I discuss the four types of teamwork in nature.

Where you a have a very large group or a crowd, it is only possible to achieve coordinated action if each member does the same thing at the same time. Thus a crowd can move a stone or excavate a hole but large scale innovation is another thing altogether (see the later chapter on 'Mass collaboration'). So large groups enable scale, mass, reach and range.

However, in a small group each member can meaningfully do different things at the same time. In other words, "Division of labor" and complex coordination. So a small group may not be able to lift a large weight but it could design a clever tool to make lifting that weight much easier.

So nature shows us the importance of having the right group size for the job at hand. It also shows us that "one size does not fit all," in terms of groups, by its ability to have all sizes of interconnected groups. For example, in the ant world we have castes within colonies, within food webs, within ecosystems.

A critical point for human teams is that they need to allow members to enjoy both the small group dynamic for innovation, and the large group dynamic for scale.

Clustering

Engaging the many through the few

Nature's networks are clustered. The technical term for this is "scale-free networks." In simple terms, what this means is that in most naturally occurring networks some of the nodes have many more connections than the average.

This makes sense instinctively. For example, some of our friends seem to know everybody. If we need to reach someone we don't directly know, we might try them first. This structure also describes the neurons in the brain and other emerging social structures such as the 'hub' sites that are the best connected on the Internet.

What this means for teams is that if you are lucky some of your team members will have extreme connectivity in terms of relationships. The team needs to take advantage of these existing connections rather than try and have the team leader(s) create and manage new connections from scratch.

These highly connected people are described elsewhere in various terms, including "alpha users," "connectors" and "influentials." But no matter what they are called, if they are well managed and motivated they can provide the most efficient and effective channels for the team to engage with its wider community.

Chapter Summary

Nature's teams display four traits that don't naturally seem to occur in organizational teams and that I contend would make a huge difference to their performance:

1. *Collective Leadership.* Any group member can take the lead.
2. *Instant Messaging.* Instant whole-group broadcast communications.
3. *Ecosystems.* Small is Beautiful …..but Big is Powerful.
4. *Clustering.* Engaging the many through the few.

This chapter is only a quick snapshot of how biological teams operate. We will develop these ideas in much more detail in "Part 2. Bioteaming: The Detailed Model."

4. How can we do better than nature's teams?

Intelligence and Autonomy

There are two obvious differences between biological and human teams, *intelligence* and *autonomy*.

Human teams have vastly superior intelligence to biological teams and much greater potential for autonomous behavior by individual members. Let's look at each one in turn.

The Intelligence Factor. Vastly superior team member intelligence, perhaps surprisingly, does not actually make a significant difference to how successful a team can be.

Since bioteaming, as I will show, is based on a distributed intelligence model, what really counts is the ability for the team to use its intellectual capabilities in a collective, collaborative and cooperative fashion. So while bioteams CAN easily accommodate highly intelligent team members, they do not generally require them.

What is strategically important, for operating as efficiently as a bioteam, is the ability of team members to be able to self-select when to utilize personal "intelligence" and critical thinking, and when to rely on team intelligence.

The Autonomy Factor. Autonomy defines the ability of team members to choose what action to take in response to a given stimulus. More importantly, autonomy provides individual team members the freedom to choose how quickly, and with what degree of commitment or force, they can act. Biological teams (except for highly intelligent ones such as groups of primates or dolphins), automatically make a pre-determined response, without consideration or delay, when receiving a recognized stimulus.

In biological teams there is usually no cognitive process between stimulus received and response made.

In human teams there is something between stimulus and response: Free Will, Choice. The philosophical importance of a person being able to control the response they make to a stimulus was extensively developed by Viktor Frankl (in the concept of

Logotheraphy) from his experiences as a prisoner and psychiatrist in Nazi concentration camps in the second world war. [1]

The impact of individual team beliefs on overall performance

How we will act is influenced by the beliefs we hold, regarding the situation we find ourselves in, when we receive the stimulus. For example, if I do not feel I am being adequately supported or appreciated by the rest of the team, I may avoid action where there is a perceived risk of my failure.

Alternatively, if I feel fully supported I might take bigger risks. In simple terms, human teams have to address the critical issue of team member motivation, whereas biological teams do not.

Effective bioteaming cannot be achieved in an organizational team that is suffering from poor motivation. This is why, to be really effective, a human bioteam must also take into account the team's beliefs and the motivations of its highly intelligent and autonomous members.

Unfortunately there is very little research about the impact of team member beliefs on overall team performance. The only study that partly addresses this issue is the unique work on "Learned Optimism," by Professor Martin Seligman. [2]

Dr Seligman is a clinical psychologist who for the last twenty years has studied the areas of learned optimism and also 'learned helplessness, to help individuals deal with depression and pessimism in their lives. As a sub-topic within his research, Dr. Seligman has explored how optimism and pessimism in team members impacts the overall team performance. According to Dr. Seligman's research, optimistic teams will recover more easily from setbacks than pessimistic ones; this does not vary with differing levels of team members' skills and intelligence.

Uncovering the "hidden beliefs" of high performing teams

From a review of the literature and original research I have identified seven beliefs that I will argue make a huge difference to a teams performance:

1. Clear and Public Accountability
2. Trusted Competency
3. Give and Take
4. Total Transparency

5. Shared Glory
6. Meaningful Mission Value
7. Outcome Optimism

Chapter Summary

Humans have much greater autonomy and intelligence than animals. In addition we have belief systems that can both motivate and demotivate us, and consequently make a huge difference to our performance in a team, independent of how it is organized. I propose that Bioteaming includes identifying your team's beliefs and will explore Team Beliefs in Bioteaming more fully in a later chapter, "Uncovering the hidden beliefs of High Performing Teams."

5. An Overview of Bioteaming

There are three major components of bioteaming:
1. Team Beliefs
2. Bioteam Action Zones and Rules
3. Bioteam Techniques

I introduced team beliefs in the previous section and will cover it in detail in "Uncovering the hidden beliefs of High Performing Teams." I will cover the techniques in a dedicated section – "Key Bioteaming Techniques."

In this section I want to introduce the four bioteaming action zones that group the 12 bioteaming action rules:
1. *Leadership zone*: Treat every team member as a leader
2. *Connectivity zone*. Connect team members, partners and networks synergistically
3. *Execution zone*. Experiment, cooperate and learn
4. *Organization zone*. Establish sustainable self-organization

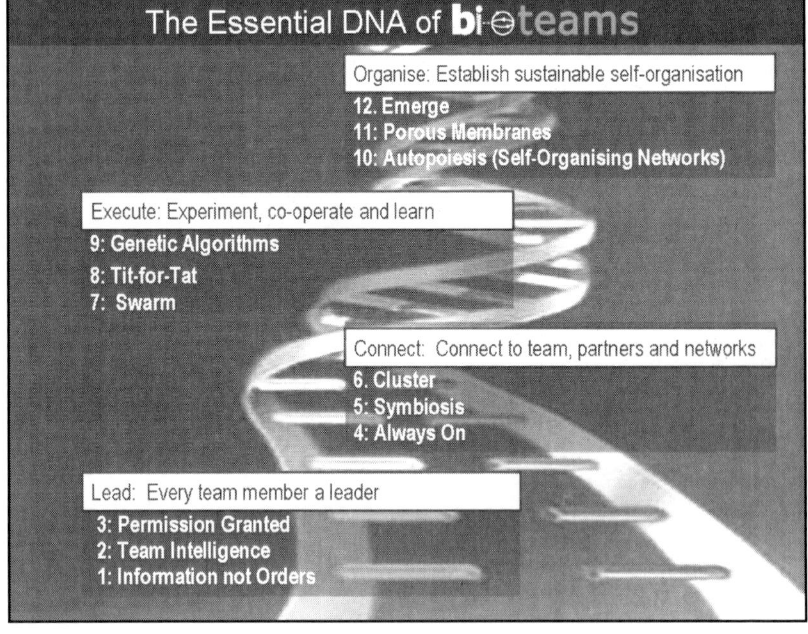

The four action zones are to a bioteam what the four chemical bases (A, T, G and C) are to DNA. Their interdependencies and constantly repeating patterns provide the building blocks of the double helix structure common to all living things. There are 12 rules in bioteams, three per bioteam zone:

Bioteams Leadership Zone

Bioteaming trait: Treat every team member as a leader.

Rule 1: Stop Controlling

Communicate information not orders

Traditional teams issue orders and use two-way communications widely. Bioteams provide "situational information" to the team members who are trained to judge themselves what they should do in the best interests of the team. They move exceptionally fast because they mostly use *one-way broadcast communications* and use two-way communications only when necessary.

Rule 2: Team Intelligence

Mobilize everyone to look for and manage team threats and opportunities

In traditional teams, it's the leader's job to provide most of the "Team Intelligence," information on potential threats to, or opportunities for, the team. In a Bioteam, it is every team member's responsibility to constantly look-out for relevant *team intelligence* and to ensure it is instantly communicated to all other team members through a small but complete set of message protocols.

Rule 3: Permission Granted

Achieve accountability through transparency not permission

Traditional teams protect themselves against *member mistakes* by establishing layers of permission that must be granted before a team member may take action in certain circumstances. We call these *"Permission Structures."*

Bioteams slash down these "Permission Structures" to the absolute bare minimum. The only permission structures kept in place by a bioteam are those needed to protect the team against the potentially critical mistakes that would threaten the sustainability of the bioteam's own mission. *Accountability* in bioteams is achieved through "team transparency" and "reputation-based" systems, not through control and hierarchical authorization systems.

Bioteams Connectivity Zone

Bioteaming trait: Connect team members, partners and networks synergistically

Rule 4: Always-On

*Provide 24*7 instant "in-situ" message hotlines for all team members*

Traditional teams expect their members to go somewhere, such as their PC, to *get their messages*. Bioteams "take the messages to the team members" via whichever device suits each individual member best at any particular time in their working day.

Rule 5: Symbiosis

Treat external partners as fully trusted team members

Traditional teams pay 'lip-service' to team members from external organizations, such as customers or suppliers, in terms of *transparency and trust*. Bioteams pick their partners very carefully but once they have committed to them they treat them identical to their own internal team members by *granting them full transparency and trust*.

Rule 6: Cluster

Nurture the team's internal and external networks and connections

Traditional Teams don't think about their networks – they believe it's the team leader's job to make sure they have all the necessary resources.

Bioteams pay a lot of attention to the *collective networks* and relationships of each team member. This is to ensure they have adequate *"strong ties"* to get the work done well and that they can *'call in short-notice favors'* as needed from external parties.

These networking relationships ensure bioteams have sufficient *"weak ties"* to quickly receive and identify early warning signals, news, rumors and hard to access information. This helps them to anticipate important changes from the external marketplaces in which they operate.

Bioteams Execution Zone

Bioteaming trait: Experiment, cooperate and learn

Rule 7: Swarm

Develop consistent autonomous team member behaviors

Traditional teams focus on team member individuality as a means of achieving creativity and innovation but neglect the *hidden power* of consistent member behaviors. Bioteams have discovered that, for a team to be really effective, it is critical to count on the ability of the team to guarantee a pre-defined set of key tasks in a reliable and systematic fashion. This requires that team members are competent and aware of what the fundamental requirements are, and that each one of the team members is willing, and capable of attending to these fundamental duties when needed. Bioteam members take a proactive and responsible interest in anything that might affect the ultimate success of their project whether it's *within their defined project role or not.*

Rule 8: Tit-for-Tat

Team members must learn effective biological and interpersonal cooperation strategies

Traditional teams try to play *"Win-Win"* and *"Collaborate"* but don't actually have any practical strategies or tactics for achieving this. Traditional teams are not really interested in the *real, often raw, basic and undeclared, motivations of their teammates.*

Bioteams realize that *"Win-Win" is an outcome, not a strategy*, and use nature's proven personal collaboration strategies to create the conditions for it to happen. Bioteam personal collaboration strategies also address the *"What's in it for me?"* question for each team member.

Rule 9: Genetic Algorithms

Learn through experimentation, mutation and team review

Traditional teams believe that *analysis is the best way to get things right.* Consequently, they engage in extensive planning, design and preparation tasks before trying out new things or releasing new products to their customers.

Bioteams believe that *"live controlled experimentation"* is the only way to get things right and that most things won't work out as planned anyway, no matter how well they are analyzed and designed. Bioteams quickly experiment with multiple alternative courses of action, often in parallel and in progressively larger increments to find out what works best. After they have collected sufficient data they build on and methodically apply the most promising results.

Bioteams Organization Zone

Bioteaming trait: Establish sustainable self-organization

Rule 10: Self-Organizing Networks

Define the team in terms of "network transformations" – not outputs

Traditional teams define their goals and roles in terms of the outputs and activities they are expected to produce, *i.e., inanimate objects.* Bioteams define their *goals and roles* in terms of the *transformations* they intend to make in the people and partners they will engage with, *i.e., living things.* They are change agents by definition.

Rule 11: Porous Membranes

Develop team boundaries that are open to energy but closed to waste

In a traditional team, the leader selects the members, and the team effectively becomes "sealed" at the pre-ordained "right size," in terms of members very early in its lifecycle. There is a big focus on full-time members as the team's "product engines." *In a bioteam the members select the members* and recognize that the "right team size" will only emerge over time, no matter what the plan says.

Bioteams keep looking for new, useful team members throughout their team life-span. Bioteams particularly seek out part-time members, advisors, experts, "jungle-guides" and external allies who can help them just-in-time as necessary.

Rule 12: Emerge

Scale naturally through nature's universal growth and decay cycles

Traditional teams grow as quick as they can to the agreed size and as per the agreed project schedule.

Bioteams are aware that growth is not something that can be managed or controlled. The team leaders and members treat their own bioteam like it is a "living thing" and watch for and facilitate natural opportunities for its growth.

Chapter Summary

I have identified 12 bioteaming rules to enable an organizational team to operate more biologically:

Rule 1: Stop Controlling
Communicate information not orders

Rule 2: Team Intelligence
Mobilize everyone to look for and manage team threats and opportunities

Rule 3: Permission Granted
Achieve accountability through transparency not permission

Rule 4: Always-On
*Provide 24*7 instant "in-situ" message hotlines for all team members*

Rule 5: Symbiosis
Treat external partners as fully trusted team members

Rule 6. Cluster
Nurture the team's internal and external networks and connections

Rule 7: Swarm
Develop consistent autonomous team member behaviors

Rule 8: Tit-for-Tat
Team members must learn effective biological and interpersonal cooperation strategies

Rule 9: Genetic Algorithms
Learn through experimentation, mutation and team review

Rule 10: Self-Organizing Networks
Define the team in terms of "network transformations" – not outputs

Rule 11: Porous Membranes
Develop team boundaries that are open to energy but closed to waste

Rule 12. Emerge
Scale naturally through nature's universal growth and decay cycles

I explore each of these rules further in "Part 2: Bioteaming The Detailed Model."

6. Birds do it and great teams do it, too

When I started to examine great teams in different domains such as business, government, voluntary sector and sports I was fascinated to discover that many of them are already using different aspects of bioteaming.

Bioteaming is, of course, a new discipline so these teams, and they were improving their performance under different banners such as:

- Self-Managed Teams
- Self-Organizing Groups
- High Performing Teams
- Complex Adaptive Systems

In the case studies section of the book you will find the stories of a number of organizations that have used bioteams *explicitly*. But in this section, I will introduce you to some of the great teams that are *implicitly* bioteaming.

Great Enterprises do it

Capital One Bank

In *The Biology of Business* [3], a chapter is dedicated to Capital One, the highly innovative credit card company. Capital One's approach to organizing its teams is *highly biological,* for example:

1. *Swarming (i.e., Rapid Deployment)* – once Capital One identify a product as a potential winner, they deploy it exceptionally quickly, and with force, to attempt to dominate and cherry pick the niche, before the competition can catch up.
2. *Autonomy* – it is everyone's job, not just the organizational leaders', to manage "organizational white space" and operate outside the traditional boundaries whenever the need arises.
3. *Rapid Evolution* – the bank conducts some 15,000 new product introductions (credit card), "experiments" per annum. Each introduction is low cost, and only 1% of them are taken

forward based on the early pilot market feedback. In other words, they have a way to make a rapid prediction of the likely value the market will place on the prospective new product, *before* costly roll-out, a kind of "market proxy."

Schlumberger

David Wessel writing for the Wall Street Journal in "Motivating Workers by giving them a vote," [4] describes the success Schlumberger had in using *online communities of practice,* with some 23 communities ranging from chemistry to oil well-engineering, supporting 140 special-interest subgroups, and involving more than 11,750 employees as members.

In multinational organizations such as Schlumberger, with thousands of employees spread all over the globe, effectively sharing knowledge, expertise and experience can be a real headache. Schlumberger attribute much of their success in this area to the decision they made to make the communities self-governing and allowing each community to elect its own leaders.

This is a key tenet of bioteaming, treat all team members as leaders and let them manage themselves through self-organizing networks operating within clear corporate ground rules.

General Electric

Jeremy Zawodny drew my attention to a Fast Company article from September 1999 called "Engines of Democracy," [5] that describes a revolutionary jet engine plant in Durham, North Carolina that produces some of General Electric's most important engines: the GE90, the CF6, and the CFM56.

The plant at Durham illustrates beautifully the power of the first rule of bioteams, treat every team member like a leader.

"GE/Durham has more than 170 employees but just one boss: the plant manager. Everyone in the place reports to her. Which means, that on a day-to-day basis the people who work here have no boss. They essentially run themselves."

"The jet engines are produced by nine teams of people – teams that are given just one basic directive: *the day that their next engine must be loaded onto a truck*. All other decisions, like who does what work; how to balance training, vacations, overtime against work flow; how to make the manufacturing process more efficient; how to handle teammates who slack off; stay within the team."

The results are very impressive: Although comparisons between GE plants are difficult, no two plants do exactly the same kind of work, with exactly the same kind of overhead to support it. Bob McEwan, who has authority over GE/Durham says simply, "They are the best in the GE Aircraft Engines division."

Southwest Airlines

In "Trusting a community to get it right," [6] Scott Gatz observes the way Southwest Airlines use self-organization in their passenger queuing systems. This highlights a major trait of bioteams, Symbiosis. This simply means including your customers as full partners within your team. This is a major head shift for many enterprises, traditionally customers are outside the team serving them.

"You might think that the SWA gates would be a madhouse, but in fact they are very orderly. People arrive and begin to line-up into three lines (A, B and C) in a quite orderly fashion. People in each row are cordial to each other asking, "is this the line for B to San Diego?" and exchanging niceties and often that question allows people to break into a friendly conversation. If you were to look at the gate area from above, you'd see what looks like three branches on a tree, they curve around the furniture and the walls, but they are a line."

Scott contrasts the Southwest Airlines experience with the one most travelers would be familiar with at America West: "A throng of people surrounded the doorway to their gate, each trying to push past each other so they could get to their seat earlier (even though they know they are guaranteed to sit in the same seat no matter how quickly they board)."

Great Organizations do it

Humberside Training and Enterprise Council (TEC)

Peter Fryer was Chief Executive of the Humberside Training and Enterprise Council (TEC) in the UK from 1991 – 2001 and is a pioneer in introducing the principles of complexity and self-managed teams to organizations. [7]

Peter believes passionately that most organizational processes are written because their leaders are not prepared to address the more fundamental question: "Can you trust your staff to behave like responsible adults or not?"

Conversations with Peter inspired some of my initial thoughts on the whole problem of "permission structures" in teams. Subsequently, I discovered that nature's teams don't have permission structures, orders or "command and control" leadership styles, that's why they are so agile and responsive.

In "An organization case study in complex adaptive systems," Peter describes how his work at Humberside TEC was guided by three core principles:

1. Let the organization operate naturally.
2. Enrich and increase connections.
3. Enhance feedback.

Peter explains how these core principles were used to develop a learning organization where: "Staff can take ownership of the organization resulting in the development of a thriving community, where innovation flourishes and where traditional results improve and costs fall."

9-11 Crisis Response Team

Dr. Will Marling, Interim Executive Director, National Organization for Victim Assistance (NOVA), describes how he participated in a crisis response team to establish a Family Assistance Center in Liberty State Park just across the Hudson River from Downtown Manhattan and the World Trade Center site in response to 9-11.

The team evolved a biological approach to sharing information in real time, using mobile phones, that illustrates the bioteams rules *"Always on"* and *"Team Intelligence."* Will describes the unfurling drama: "Within hours of planes hitting the World Trade Center, I was on the phone with other crisis responders. I was part of a network that had been trained in crisis intervention by NOVA. As commercial aircraft were still grounded, within the week I was in a van with other responders, heading toward New York City.

"As with any disaster, communication was essential as plans and resources had to be adapted by the minute. One of the first allocations was cellular phones. Mobile transmitters were brought in and the team members were assigned phones. From that point, roles had to be assigned. The NOVA network would be providing over six hundred volunteers over the next few months that would be 'companions' to victims walking through the maze of services provided at the Family Assistance Center."

"What was clear early on, and then continuing through the process of providing victim assistance through companioning, is the significance of effective sharing of information. The size of the location and the nature of the logistics meant that the team was continually separated. There were times when various approaches to information were needed. Sometimes it was 'for your information' notifications like, 'DNA trailer will close at 5pm today.' Other times, responses were needed as in 'Staff meeting at HQ, 6am. Can you be present?'"

Looking back on the experience with hindsight, Will reflects: "We had a team leader and in the crisis management model, there is a hierarchy for chain-of-command. But our work as a team had to be more organic because we had to function in a situation none of us had been in before. We had to work around certain principles of continual communication and team intelligence. When we focused on the natural processes for communication and relationship, we were clearly most effective in our purpose for being there: serving the victims of 9-11."

Great Networks and Supply Chains do it

Boeing

July 08, 2007 Boeing officially debuted the technologically advanced, and environmentally progressive, 787 Dreamliner in a celebration attended by employees, airline customers, supplier partners and government and community officials. The 787 Premiere potentially reached 100 million or more viewers, making it one of the largest corporate TV and Internet broadcasts in history.

Boeing, competing in a world-class industry undergoing massive, rapid transformation, knew that they needed a radically different business model for building the 787. They chose a networked supplier-partner model involving 70 partners and 72 different sites around the world.

According to Mike Bair, Boeing Commercial Airplanes vice president/general manager of the 787 program, reported in "Boeing Celebrates the Premiere of the 787 Dreamliner," "Our journey began some six years ago when we knew we were on the cusp of delivering valuable technologies that would make an economic difference to our airline customers. In our business, that happens every 15 or so years, so we have to get it right." [8]

The change in mindset from suppliers to partners is nowhere better illustrated than in Boeing's website for the 787 (newairplane.com/787/), where a section entitled "Who is building the 787" invites you to click on the fuselage of the plane to see which partner is building each system and component.

With Southwest airlines we saw one side of Symbiosis, how they treated their customers as full members of their team. Boeing's Dreamliner illustrates the other side of Symbiosis, treating your suppliers as full partners in your team. Traditional command and control models do not deliver the levels of agility and responsiveness needed in today's supply chains to deliver world-class product to critical market windows.

The film industry

In an excellent paper, "The Virtual Organization – Technical or Social Innovation? Lessons from the Film Industry," [9] Lucas Introna, Hope Moore and Mike Cushman from the London School of Economics explore the parallels and the lessons we can adapt from the film industry in attempting to improve our organizational teams. They suggest that: "The film production process is characterized by flexible adaptation to changing production conditions, and illustrates the balance of flexibility and hierarchy that is required between contracted individuals who are involved in collaborative, creative, short-term contracts."

They conclude that we can gain a lot of insight into how to improve teams by using ideas from the film production process particularly:

- Roles, power and lightweight contracts
- Reputation, norms and moral sanctions
- Common Language (Filmspeak)

- Networks of trusted partners

These are all important bioteaming characteristics. For example, in bioteams "moral sanctions" are central, based on the 'Tit for Tat' principle [21, 28] and reputation replaces authority as the ultimate motivator of bioteaming performance.

Great Causes do it

Open Source Software

Brian Teeman, in an excellent paper "Roles and responsibilities of users and community members in an open source project," [10] describes the inner workings of an open source software (OSS) development project based on his experience in developing the Mambo product.

OSS has been a shining example of how it is possible for teams, whose members may not ever meet, to work together without direct financial incentive and still produce top quality software products. Three things are very clear from Brian's account of OSS teams:

1. *Personal motivations* are explicit for every team member
2. All work is voluntary and the *leader cannot give orders*
3. Each project passionately nurtures its *network of supporters*

These principles align exactly with the three bioteam rules "Tit for Tat," "Stop Controlling" and "Cluster."

Smart Mobs

Smart Mobs is a major emerging social group phenomenon defined by Wikipedia as: a form of self-structuring social organization through technology-mediated, intelligent "emergent behavior." The concept was introduced by Howard Rheingold in his book *Smart Mobs: The Next Social Revolution.* [11]

Robin Good in "Online Activism: Media Stereotypes And The Rise Of Smart Mobs" [12] goes on to explain: "The news has been turned upside down by citizen journalism, and the mobile army of camera-phone owning street reporters. Education has spilled over from the academy and into virtual worlds and other informal spaces. Film and media-making has started to tap into the creative potential of the people formerly known as the audience. And then there's politics. Politics is no longer something enacted by other people on our behalf from a safe distance, or at least, it no longer has to be."

In "Four examples for innovative mobile phone use in Africa," [13] *Christian Kreutz blogs about* examples of highly creative use of mobile phones in Africa for news reporting, and social change. "Mobile reporters can now potentially report from all corners of Africa. The project is a cooperation between skoeps.com (a Dutch mobile reporting portal) and the Africa Interactive Media Foundation. Most articles have a "blogging character," deliver intriguing stories, and report about all kinds of topics. Mobile phones are used to write the articles by using an additional keyboard and film material. It is amazing to see how mobile phones are used to film interviews, give the impressions through photos, and write stories."

This illustrates very well the Smart Mobs concept and the power of all members of a team being on the look out for useful information. I call it the principle of 'team intelligence' based on how biological groups such as ants and bees forage. It provides a team with a highly effective distributed early warning system. When this is combined with the principle of "always on" and powered through mobile phones the results can be startling.

Great Sports Teams do it

The Boston Red Sox

Dave Cooper, a sports consultant with ML Sports Management in Toronto, works to optimize the performance of sports teams. Dave observes that great baseball teams like the Boston Red Sox, which recently won the baseball World Series, don't just have leader but many leaders, each in different aspects of the game. These leaders send consistent short messages, just like ant pheromones or bee waggle dances!

"As in all successful team experiences the leader builds the culture and has certain players he trusts to take on ownership of that culture. In Boston's case they had team Captain and catcher

Jason Varitek, Josh Beckett, David Ortiz."

"Veritek, was the backbone of the team. He was the "Captain" who maintained the level of performance from his teammates that he knew would be necessary to be successful. Pitcher Josh Beckett was one of the best pitchers in the league and yet maintained a strenuous work ethic and desire to be the best he could be, sending a consistent message to his teammates of what would be expected to be successful. Designated hitter, David Ortiz was the player who gave his team the confidence they could succeed when the going gets tough."

"When you have these underlying consistent messages being sent, a foundation is established where younger players or player new to the team feel comfortable and recognize that their talents and role in the team is important. We saw this with the Red Sox, by big play after big play from players such as pitcher Jon Lester, and infielders Dustin Pedroia and Kevin Youkilis."

Dave sums it up like this: "Teams that win have an uncanny way to recognize big situations and have the confidence to perform under pressure. In my opinion, this only happens through the leaders sending a consistent message of what is expected and making sure everyone knows that their talents and skills are needed to maximize their team's potential to succeed!"

Great Soccer Teams

One of the common attributes of many great soccer teams is the fact that they seem to have not one but multiple leaders both on and off the pitch. There could not be a greater contrast between a great soccer team and a traditional command and control organizational team.

Coaches refer to the "Team Backbone," which is essentially a chain that runs from the goalkeeper through the defense, through the midfield to the forward line and typically consists of four or five players. These players are viewed as the collective leadership team on the pitch.

Recently there has been much debate in England on the difference between the national team of 1966 that won the World Cup, and the current national team that is seen as possessing a number of immensely talented individuals but is a huge underachiever as a team in terms of major tournament wins. A recurring point made by many fans is that the older team had a number of "talkers" on the pitch who would constantly motivate or chastise their team members as required. This is the bioteams concept of short messages that can be originated by any team member and are direct and sharp and instant.

Soccer teams also illustrate well the concept of Swarming – an automatic, instant, consistent response being required from each member whenever a certain type of threat or opportunity presents itself.

Northern Ireland's Soccer Team

Northern Ireland's soccer team set a record in January 2004, but it's one nobody is proud of. The team went 10 games in International football without even scoring a goal, never mind winning, and dropped to their lowest ever FIFA ranking of 122nd (FIFA are the world governing body for soccer).

Fast forward on a few years to November 2007 and everything has changed. Northern Ireland, a very small country with a population of just 1.5 million, is now ranked the 36th best soccer team in the world on the back of some quite amazing victories summarized in the table below:

Opponent	Date	Result	Population	FIFA Ranking
England	Sept 2005	WON 1-0	40M	11
Spain	Sept 2006	WON 3-2	40M	6
Sweden	March 2007	WON 2-1	9M	24
Denmark	Nov 2007	WON 2-1	5M	29

But the team is largely made up of the same players who created the record for the most games without a goal. So what has changed?

First, a new set of beliefs; Lawrie Sanchez, the manager of the team shares his views of the importance of team beliefs: "I would tell my players that I have played with a bloke who always thought he was the best player on the field whether he was playing against Bryan Robson or Alan Shearer," he says "And I tell them that now he is in Hollywood, if he walks on to a movie set with Robert De Niro, he thinks he's the better actor. It just shows what belief in yourself can do."

Second, a different team organization approach that maximized the (limited) talent to its full: "With all managers the team has got to be more important (than individuals), but at the top clubs the game is about having some massive players who satisfy the crowd."

Olympic Rowing Crews

On Saturday 21st August 2004 at the Athens Olympic Games, Matthew Pinsent, CBE, entered Olympic history. In one of the classic sporting moments of all time, he led Great Britain to victory over the Canadian World Champions by just eight one hundredths of a second, and also won his fourth Olympic Gold medal!

When Matthew talks about the teamwork in world-class rowing teams he stresses the importance of two vital bioteaming concepts: collective *leadership* and swarming.

- *Distributed leadership.* The rowers are all facing the wrong direction and the cox is the only one who can see whether the team is taking the correct line or not. The cox may have the least glamorous position and may lack the physical power of the other team members, but without the cox the teams trust they cannot win. The cox would not be considered the overall leader but like all high performing teams will be totally trusted to be a leader in certain domains.
- *Swarming – Synchronized team member response.* Somebody rowing too fast is as bad as somebody rowing too slow in terms of disrupting the overall speed of the boat. The team need to be synchronized, it is not about everybody doing things as fast or as well as they can. It is about everybody being coordinated! This is one of the best lessons we can learn from nature's teams, Swarming: a synchronized member response is much better than individual response in certain critical situations.

7. The state of Bioteaming

Dr. R. Meredith Belbin

Dr. R. Meredith Belbin, regarded as the father of "team-role" theory and one of the world's foremost experts on teams, predicts that our organizational teams will evolve into more biologically inspired forms. Specifically, Belbin suggests our organizations will evolve into teams "that combine the devolved but integrated strengths of the higher insects with the directive and strategic abilities of humans."

In his book *The Coming Shape of Organization* [14] he picks out five things human teams need to learn from "a diminutive master-class" of social insects such as bees, ants and termites:

1. *Division of Labor.* They have no overall single leader but rather a cooperating leadership caste.
2. *Superior use of Intelligence.* Social insects are superior to humans in their ability to rapidly integrate new information from a wide range of senses and share it widely, to ensure urgent action happens immediately, rather than passing it up and down the hierarchical chains of command.
3. *Flexibility of Member Castes.* Social insect colonies consist of a number of distinct castes of insects playing specialized roles such as foragers, attackers and nest maintainers. However these castes are flexible and grow and shrink as required and can even change their roles in a crisis.
4. *Devolved decision making.* The system is geared up to concurrent (as opposed to sequential) decision making – there is no chain of command to slow decisions down.
5. *Redundancy and Contingency.* Colonies are not dependent on a single individual or system. They are based on scale and interlocking systems, any one of which might fail without catastrophic consequences for the colony.

Belbin goes on to identify two priority guidelines that he suggests seem worth transferring immediately to human affairs:

- Transferring major decision making away from a single boss (Mr. Big) to a cooperating leadership group.

- Replacing monolithic organizational processes with concurrent interlinked systems.

In a statement that seems to lay down a challenge to humility in our thinking about teams, Belbin concludes that "evolution will almost inevitably take us in the direction of species that have arrived at superior forms of organization before us."

Global Interest in Bioteaming

I have been engaging with the global community of team collaboration practitioners, leaders, coaches and academics on the emerging topic of bioteams since May 2005 through my bioteams blog, www.bioteams.com, and my Bumblebee persona.

To establish where the hot spots of interest and engagement were, in the summer of 2007, I incorporated a facility on the blog to track where visitors were coming from. The results were astonishing, with over 100,000 visits in five months, from almost every country in the world, suggesting a global fascination with the concept of bioteaming.

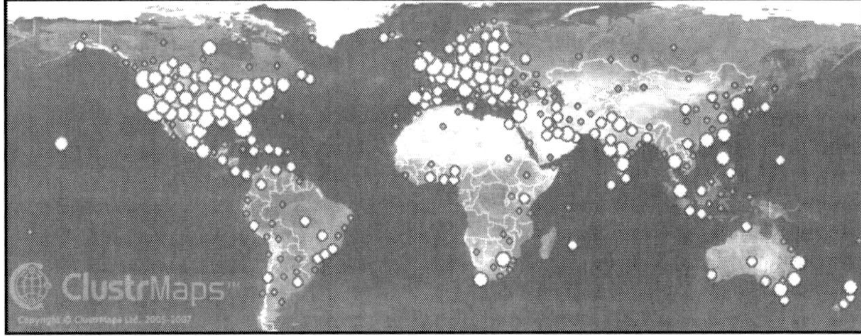

As expected the most developed regions, particularly the US and Europe, are leading the way. However, what is truly inspiring is the level of interest from eastern cultures and the less developed regions. The figure above shows clearly that interest in learning from nature's best teams transcends cultures, geographies and technology maturity.

Bioteaming really does seem to be an emergent, global phenomenon. Summary traffic maps for www.bioteams.com can be viewed at http://tinyurl.com/ytshqg

Part 2: Bioteaming – The Detailed Model

8. Hidden beliefs of high performing teams

From what we have been able to find there is no other research in the public domain that directly looks at the beliefs of *team members* in high performance teams. There is, however, excellent material on the detailed characteristics and behaviors of high performing teams. Two books include *Hot Groups: Seeding Them, Feeding Them, and Using Them to Ignite Your Organization,* by Lipman-Blumen and Leavitt; [15] and *Organizing Genius: The Secrets of Creative Collaboration,* by Bennie and Lieberman. [16]

According to my own personal experience and the research (see "High Performing Teams Beliefs Research" in this chapter) I carried out on this topic, High Performing Teams (HPT) are *immediately* identifiable by the tacit, or hidden beliefs by which their general behavior and attitude is determined.

Belief 1. Clear and Public Accountability

HPT members believe that every member of the team has a clear and public accountability. Every team member knows what she/he is responsible for, and what she/he can count on the others for.

Belief 2. Trusted Competency

HPT members believe that the rest of the team trusts them to know how to do their job properly without being supervised. In a multidisciplinary team this translates into "I know what you have to do and am confident you can do it. How you do it is your business."

Belief 3. Give and Take

HPT members believe that if they need help they can ask for it and it will be freely offered. They believe that asking for help, with moderation, actually increases their standing within the team rather than diminishing it. They also believe something is wrong if somebody is struggling along and not asking for help, or is asking for help but being ignored by the rest of the team.

Belief 4. Total Transparency

HPT members expect to be kept appraised in an honest and timely manner of any important issues in the project even if the issue does not directly affect them. This is part of the dynamic of every member believing in themselves to share team leader responsibilities; therefore becoming capable of contributions beyond the ones normally dictated by their specific team role. HPT members also believe that individual team members should be free to pass opinions about situations they are not directly responsible for, and that these opinions should always be highly respected and listened to.

Belief 5. Shared Glory

HPT members believe they are all in it together and that glory and pain will be shared. Like the four musketeers, it is *"One for all and all for one."* HPT members do not believe that their leader will take an unfairly big portion of the credit for a success, or all of the blame for a failure. Underpinning this is the belief that each team member is equally accountable to the leader and fellow team members.

Belief 6. Meaningful Mission Value

HPT members believe that the group's operational mission is significant, important and meaningful. They believe that if they are successful they will have made a fundamental contribution to their organization and possibly to the greater good. If they saw the project as just 'business as usual' or routine, then their motivation would sag significantly. To foster this sentiment, the task must not seem trivial or easy or as if it has been done before. HPT members also generally feel they are the only people in the organization who could succeed at accomplishing such a difficult task.

Belief 7. Outcome Optimism

Finally, as discussed under "Learned Optimism" [2] HPT members are confident that they (and often, they alone) will succeed in delivering the mission of the project.

Good beliefs make a team work harder

One of the main consequences of nurturing a team to develop a deeply shared set of beliefs is a greater commitment by individual members to put in the necessary amount of work for the project to succeed. If the team feels trusted, it acquires self-confidence and adopts a meaningful and responsible attitude toward realizing the mission successfully.

Bioteaming includes identifying your team's beliefs

The first step to an ambitious virtual networked business team is to try to honestly identify the current beliefs that each individual team members hold. Next, this set of beliefs can be compared with the seven "hidden," high performance beliefs reviewed above, to identify the most appropriate team motivational drivers.

As is true for all beliefs, people can only be encouraged to modify them. It is next to impossible to mandate their change unless it is the fruit of an individual, conscious and voluntary decision. The most powerful techniques for modifying beliefs are those that excel at illustrating the consequences of existing beliefs, while showcasing the profiles and characteristics of alternative beliefs. Such responsibilities would generally be delegated to the senior and more experienced members of the team.

High Performing Teams Beliefs Research

As part of the process to validate the beliefs of Bioteams we conducted a short research project on the beliefs of three High Performing Teams (HPTs) in a global software organization. Our research indicated that four beliefs were universally held: clear and public accountability, trusted competency, give and take and outcome optimism. Five other beliefs were largely or partially held suggesting that an HPT may have between 4 and 9 key beliefs.

Background and Context

The project identified a number of High Performing Teams

within the software organization. We surveyed those HPTs to determine their beliefs. We carried this out by asking them questions in ten areas of belief. These ten areas had been determined as possible HPT key belief areas from a review of the relevant literature.

We conducted two surveys: the first (using Microsoft Excel) included twenty questions that allowed us to cover the 10 areas with two questions per area. This allowed a positive and a negative question to avoid "leading" the responders into the perceived correct answers.

In the second questionnaire (administered via Zap Survey), we used just ten questions and administered the questionnaire a couple of weeks after the collection of the first survey responses.

There were no significant differences between the results produced by the long (20 questions) and short questionnaires (10 questions). The ten areas we explored were as follows:

1. Clear and public accountability
2. Trusted competency
3. Give and take
4. Total transparency
5. Shared glory
6. Meaningful mission value
7. Outcome optimism
8. Success in spite of
9. Work is its own reward
10. Simply the best

We worked with three teams and obtained responses for 10 representative members across these teams. The bulk of the team members were based in the US and the rest in Europe. The teams considered that they were quite active users of "virtual team technologies" (60%). The major output of the three teams was software products. All three teams were considered HPTs by their organizational executives.

Summary of the research results

All the three teams held in common, the following beliefs:

- Q1 (clear and public accountability) – 100% agree

- Q2 (trusted competency) – 100% agree
- Q3 (give and take) – 100% agree
- Q7 (outcome optimism) – 100% agree

The 3 teams strongly did NOT hold the following belief:

- Q8 (success in spite of) – 100% disagree

The 3 teams generally held the following beliefs:

- Q4 (total transparency) – 80% agree
- Q9 (work is its own reward) – 80% agree

The 3 teams partially held the following beliefs but to a lesser extent:

- Q6 (meaningful mission value) – 50% agree
- Q5 (shared glory) – 60% agree
- Q10 (simply the best) – 40% agree

Note that the questions were all on the standard 5-point scale. To convert them to a single percentage, for simplicity, we ignored the midpoint % ('not sure') and subtracted the combined low points (4 and 5) percentages from the combined high points (1 and 2) percentages, e.g., 1=60%, 2=10%, 3=10%, 4=20%, 5=0% translates to (60+10) - (20) = 50%.

Conclusions we drew from these results

There were 4 beliefs that were universally held in these HPTs, 2 that were mostly held and 3 that are partially held. Thus, from this research, it looks like there are 4 to 9 beliefs of HPTs in this organization.

There is one belief that was universally not held, "success in spite of." This is very interesting in itself because some of the literature on HPTs, for example, [15] pages 67-69 and [16] pages 207-208, had suggested that such teams need to perceive a common enemy – our research does not bear this out within this organization.

This research shows that within the culture of this organization there is definitely a set of four strongly held beliefs and five generally or partially held beliefs:

Q1 (clear and public accountability) – 100% agree
Q2 (trusted competency) – 100% agree
Q3 (give and take) – 100% agree
Q7 (outcome optimism) – 100% agree
Q4 (total transparency) – 80% agree
Q9 (work is its own reward) – 80% agree
Q6 (meaningful mission value) – 50% agree
Q5 (shared glory) – 60% agree
Q10 (simply the best) – 40% agree

9. The Bioteams Leadership Zone

- ✔ All team members are Leaders.
- ✔ Use one-way and broadcast messages for all members to send and receive real-time team intelligence.

Leadership Zone: Rule 1 - Send out timely information

- ✔ Nature's teams don't issue orders.

Nature's teams broadcast information bursts and expect receiving teammates to take appropriate action – just-in-time. In Nature there exist two types of key information bursts:

- *Opportunity* information bursts and
- *Threat* information bursts.

It's all about spotting Opportunities and Threats

An example of opportunity information is where a bee spots a good nectar source and dances the waggle dance to show the other bees where it is. [17] An example of threat information is when an ant spots a predator and quickly broadcasts its presence to the other ants who will take the appropriate aggressive or defensive action. [18]

One unique trait that characterizes opportunity and threat information bursts is that they tend to be urgent. If bees don't immediately exploit the honey source just found some other insect will. If ants don't have a razor sharp response to the enemy scout they may face a potentially lethal surprise attack.

In all cases nature's teams have evolved a simple approach to communicate urgent information widely and instantly without doing anything more than sending out just-in-time information bursts and letting everyone take action in an independent fashion.

But why don't nature's teams issue orders?

The reason is that orders have higher "information complexity" than situational information and are more difficult to assemble and broadcast quickly to teammates. Orders are also more likely to contain errors and be misunderstood.

You can check this out by experimenting with work colleagues by giving out, alternatively, information bursts and "order" information. You will discover that when you give order information you inevitably have to supply considerably more situational information to ensure that the order is properly understood.

What is evident is that Nature has evolved an approach of simple message transmission coupled with enough distributed self-intelligence within each of the receivers, for being able to know what to do with it. Team members have huge amounts of locally distributed intelligence for working out the required action, given their situation.

Learning from nature means that teammates must be trained to expect information, rather than orders, and must be able to quickly work out appropriate responses without having to be told.

If we start providing just-in-time information bursts to a team that has been exposed only to receiving "orders" and "instructions" there will only be one response – team paralysis. The team members will digest the information but will not take action.

Today's organizational teams face exactly the same problems as nature's teams:

- Information needs to be communicated to all teammates quickly.
- Members of a team are generally very busy and they don't have the time to read and understand complex instructions. They need brief, synthetic, focused, short messages.

One-way is okay

When an ant or a bee broadcasts a message to another ant or bee it doesn't wait for a response.

Why?

Often times in Nature, speed is of the essence. The main reason nature's teams communicate this way is that if they waited for a response they would probably get eaten before it arrived. These insects rely on razor sharp fast responses to survive:

- Nature's teams subjugate everything to speed.

- Speed enables living animals to move to more powerful positions further up their ecosystem.
- Speed is the essential difference between the species at the top and bottom of the food chain.
- Capability for "Movement" is the defining difference between a plant and an insect or an animal.

As nature's teams are communicating information rather than orders, it follows that their communications can be broadcast rather than conversational, 2-way communication. Therefore, these messages do not need responses, as they are one-way, enabling very fast team reactions.

However, look at our organizational teams. The current school of thought is that you should generally allow, and wait for, a response to electronic communications. This style of working drastically hampers the team's speed, agility and responsiveness. Everything stops while somebody does not reply or somebody is away from his or her screen or someone's email gets bounced.

In today's organizational teams, increasing speed and responsiveness is usually *the number one challenge.*

Adopting information for action and one-way messaging is an excellent strategy for addressing this challenge.

Roger and Wilco

In aviation, there are two critical communication terms universally used in all radio transmissions, "Roger" and "Wilco." "Wilco" means I have received your message and Will Comply with it. "Roger" just means I have received your message, but I may or may not act on it.

To be a bioteam you need to find a technological way to automatically achieve "Roger" and you need to minimize all communications requiring a "Wilco." Therefore:

- Set-up and encourage your team to expect information and not orders.
- Only use two-way messages where you absolutely need to have a clear-cut response, where there is unavoidable complexity or where you require a particular bit of information.

Leadership Zone: Rule 2 - Everyone must broadcast

The Queen is Blind

Instead of issuing orders, nature's teams function by providing timely information to the team members and then expecting them to take appropriate action where needed. Surprisingly, this information is not provided by the Queen of an ant colony, but by the other members. In an ant colony the Queen's job is to reproduce, not to try to control what the other ants do.

And this is why some colonies can have up to a 300 million members while the Queen has no real idea of what each of colony members is doing at any given time. It is not the Queen bee who finds the good nectar source and dances the "waggle dance." [17] Neither is it the ant Queen who spots the ant from the rival colony out on a scouting mission. [18]

Human bioteams need to imitate nature by becoming teams of peers and leaders where every member understands that it is central to their role as a bioteam member to be on the look-out for just-in-time, critical information that may be of value to the team as a whole.

Team Vital Signs

How do you make sure team members will know what information to send out? How can you prevent them from constantly spamming other teammates with pet topics, irrelevancies and trivia? To address these problems, team members need to clearly know what is vital and what is not. To support this need, a bioteam can design a dashboard of team "vital signs" that always require immediate attention.

An analogy with medical emergencies is helpful here. Think of the vital signs for a human being: breathing, alertness, heart, pulse, and blood pressure. We need to distinguish between what signs are important, which are urgent and which are both. For example, high cholesterol is important but not urgent in the same way as a heartbeat irregularity.

So what are your team's vital signs? What changes in them require attention, and how urgent are they?

The easiest way to establish vital signs is to have the team identify and agree upon the key external and internal situations that everybody needs to pay attention to.

In other words, what are the key internal team state changes that need to be constantly monitored? For example, vital signs might include: Senior User Unhappy, Team Member Repeated Absence or Team Morale Problem.

Leadership Zone: Rule 3 – Act, don't ask (permission granted)

Permission Structures

One way organizational teams protect themselves against the risk of an individual making a critical mistake that can significantly affect the rest of the team is, using "Permission Structures." A permission structure regulates the action from taking place without some higher approval.

Nature's teams act according to their genetically programmed rules. They do not seek permission from higher authorities before acting, they just act. This is because they have little discretionary space in their individual behaviors. Also, because of the large numbers of members involved in these teams (often thousands), individual mistakes have little impact on the end result.

In human teams the effect of an individual mistake can be much more severe. Just think of the impact of a poor salesman in an enterprise, or a poor brain surgeon on a medical team.

Effective Bioteams should constantly challenge their existing "permission structures," i.e., the parts of the team's operation where an action cannot happen without somebody else's permission. On the other hand, for each of these structures, bioteams should ask – is the cost of the control greater than the cost of the potential losses if someone acts without permission?

"Act don't Ask" also raises issues of Trust in teams. It is perfectly okay to use permission structures where you don't trust a team member's *skills*. But, it is not okay to use permission structures where you don't trust a team member's *motives* or *commitment*. In these situations, you need to challenge motives and if necessary, find replacements for such team members.

Team Transparency

In technology terms, you should therefore let team members act with as much freedom as possible but ensure your technology logs all actions and who took them. This recorded information should be available to all team members (transparency). A bioteam then needs a review process where all team member actions are regularly reviewed by the whole team in the spirit of openness and learning.

The Importance of Reputation Systems

Research into self-managed teams (for example, Open Source Software Teams), [19] reveals that a major motivator for team members in the absence of 'command and control' structures is the enhancement of reputation within the group or community.

Therefore, you should try to find a way to create a mechanism where a proxy for each member's reputation can be visible and updated, by all the other team members.

There are also possibilities for the automatic accumulation of reputation, for example, through a member's responsiveness to received messages and the value other team members get from their sent messages.

10. The Bioteams Connectivity Zone

- ✔ Nurture your networks.
- ✔ Cultivate strong connections between team members, mobile communications devices, with external partners and with wider support networks.

Connectivity Zone: Rule 4 - Always On/Always Near

- ✔ The Bioteam Hotline: any member in any place can instantly reach all the other members when they need to.
- ✔ Nature's teams use few words, but they use them well and often.

Nature's teams possess a limited vocabulary of simple messages that can be broadcast by each and every member to the rest of the team in an instant. For example, Dr. Edward Wilson the world's renowned authority on Ants says: [18] "We estimate that ant species generally employ between 10 and 20 chemical words and phrases, each conveying a distinct, but very different, meaning."

So nature's teams have no "to-do" lists or in-boxes. If a message is not received and acted on immediately by the listener, then it certainly won't be done later. These 'bio-messages' have limited persistence. For example, in the case of ants a message only lasts until the scent trail evaporates.

Messages are always sent and received "in situ," i.e., a message is sent and delivered from, and to, the other team members wherever they are. Also, bioteam communication is always secondary to taking action. After sending the message, the "transmitter" immediately heads off to meet the threat or the opportunity without looking back to see if anyone else is following them.

Survival of the Fastest

The "biological hotline" provides certain advantages to nature's teams including:

- Speed of response – they can mobilize a "mass response" exceptionally quickly.
- Appropriate design – makes best use of the limited intelligence available to both transmitters and receivers.
- Minimal "down time" – the least possible time is taken up communicating, leaving the most possible time for what nature's teams are really good at – well coordinated mass action.

Organizational teams don't operate Hot-Lines

The contrast between our organizational teams and nature's teams could not be more marked:

- Nature uses simple rapidly composed *real-time messages;* we use complex precisely crafted *asynchronous documents.*
- Nature sends the message to the members; we try to get the members to go to the message (e.g., email).
- Nature emphasizes quick response; we focus on accurate communication.

In contrast, our organizational teams often:

- Are sluggish to respond
- Spend far too much time "word-smithing" complex messages (with attachments that our fellow team members at best only skim read when they return to their desks later)
- Are poor at sharing important information early ("team intelligence")

So how can we exploit the Bioteam Hotline?

First, we can differentiate between "team message situations" and "team document situations." We need both forms of communication but each at the appropriate time.

Second, just like the ants, we can define a short "vocabulary" of key message areas that should be brought instantly to everyone's immediate attention.

Third, we can construct member "personal communication profiles," telling us which device each member wants communicated through and when. The technologies offering "device presence" are particularly useful here.

Finally, we can enable "send by any and receive by all," instantaneous broadcast, and received from whichever devices team members are using.

These requirements fit well with smart mobile devices, the small screens and limited bandwidth are not a problem if you are only using simple messages and no attachments.

Benefits of "Always On/Always Near"

If we adopt this action rule we will be able to react much quicker as a team, develop a stronger sense of ownership among the whole team and have an effective 24*7 early warning system.

We are also less likely to make the mistake of confusing communicating with taking action!

Connectivity Zone: Rule 5 – Out-Team

- ✔ Bioteam Symbiosis enables close cooperative relationships between internal and external team members.

Nature collaborates to compete

A better scientific understanding of evolution achieved in the last ten years has shown that much more cooperation takes place than was originally thought in the concept, "survival of the fittest."

Competition is still crucial in nature, however, the unit of competition is as likely to be a pair of cooperating species as an individual species. Evolution is not so much competition between "lonely individuals" but between "productive partnerships."

Such collaboration is known as Symbiosis, the long-term co-evolution of two independent species for mutual gain. In Bioteaming, I call this "Out-Teaming" – embracing the outside member as a full team partner.

The scientist who has done the most to reshape our views on the symbiotic nature of evolution is Professor Lynn Margulis [20] who says, "We are symbionts on a symbiotic planet and, if we care to, we can find symbiosis everywhere."

Random mutation and *gene trading* are the two principal means for bacterial evolution. However, it was known that neither of these methods was effective in explaining the *larger forms of life*. The big question was how did these higher forms of life evolve?

This question was answered in the 1960s by *Margulis* with the discovery of *Symbiogenesis,* a third, totally unexpected avenue of evolution with profound implications for all branches of biology.

What is Symbiogenesis?

Symbiogenesis is nature's method for creating complex new species. Margulis discovered that within the more complex biological cells there is genetic material that exists outside the cell nucleus. When this material is analyzed it is clear that it has not come from the nucleus but from the DNA of other independent species. The theory suggests that in nature complex new species usually form, not by an act of independent "quantum evolution," but by the coming together and merging of two or more (less complex but independent) species.

The symbiogenesis process often starts with one species eating the other, which responds by exploiting its host as a *parasite.* Over time this combative form of symbiosis can evolve into *symbiogenesis* where the smaller species becomes forever part of the larger species, albeit maintaining its own distinct structure, but living forever inside the body of the host.

Principles of Symbiogenesis

Symbiogenesis operates on a number of important principles that can also be applied to teams:

1. *It needs time.* Symbiogenesis does not happen overnight, there needs to be a "getting to know you" period.
2. *It needs intimacy and risk-taking.* Eating and being a parasite are acts that involve intimacy and vulnerability, both parties must take the risk of disclosing and exposing to each other.
3. *It may actually come out of competition.* Symbiogenesis often starts in a *prey-predator* scenarios, don't just consider the obvious "friendly looking" partners.
4. *It needs diversity.* A cornerstone of symbiogenesis is that the two species are significantly different (often in size and function) and can be mutually advantageous to each other. So consider much more powerful and much less powerful partners than your own and also those in different areas.
5. *Three is not a crowd.* Many examples of symbiogenesis include

multiple species (e.g., Mixotricha Paradoxa is a minute amoeba made up of at least five kinds of organism). So you may "date" one partner at a time, but don't treat it as a marriage of just two parties.

Everywhere we turn in nature we see symbiotic relationships including:

- Ants and Aphids
- Crocodiles and the famous Crocodile Bird who cleans a crocodile's teeth
- Trees and nitrogen-fixing bacteria
- Birds and a multitude of Ticks
- The Bacteria and our stomachs

An important prerequisite for symbiosis is that the partners must also make an initial physical connection. In nature, this happens purely by chance. So, in nature, competition may precede collaboration, and the unit of competition is often the symbiotic pair of interdependent species.

Why does nature love symbiosis?

In nature things only survive if they provide a genetic advantage. For example, some giraffes, through genetic mutation, evolve slightly longer necks, these giraffes get to eat the better leaves on the higher branches, they become better nourished, they live longer, and they provide more and healthier young. Thus, over time, a higher percentage of the giraffe population has longer necks.

Going beyond the evolution of a single species like the giraffe, symbiosis must provide mutual benefit for it to be so dominant in nature. Two species must have a better chance of survival in partnership than in isolation.

Also, biological evolution normally proceeds at the pace of generations. On the other hand, if you have two species, each with different lifetimes, symbiosis can in effect speed up the whole process.

However, most organizational teams don't operate on the basis of symbiosis. Current wisdom is that if you are enlightened enough to have customers or partners as part of your team (most don't even go this far) you should manage (i.e., limit and control) their participation, in some way, as team members.

In current wisdom, customers or sponsors especially are not to be allowed to see the warts or to see all of the team. This lack of intimacy and lack of transparency destroys a significant portion of the potential value that a team can produce.

It also creates a lot of waste. I am sure we have all been to "pre-meetings" to prepare for meetings with the full team (including the third parties). Probably, we all have produced documents that have to be "sanitized" before they are released for full team circulation, because external staff would see them.

So what would a bioteam do?

First, we should not be naïve, we should make sure our potential partners are neither predators nor parasites (both can be equally destructive).

Second, we should have frank discussions with external team members, to identify if there are genuine areas of normal commercial difference and tension. We should not gloss over these.

Third, with the other two points addressed, we should fully embrace external team members from customer and supplier organizations as full team members and offer them full transparency. This does not necessarily mean we tell each other everything, but we should at least be transparent about where we can't be transparent!

Fourth, we should adapt proven team collaboration and rapid trust building strategies such as "Tit for Tat" [21] (See Rule 8 in the Execution Zone). This allows the inevitable failures in personal collaboration and trust to be quickly addressed without derailing the whole team.

Benefits of "Out-Teaming"

The benefits of treating external team members as full partners are obvious. It's not so obvious that out-teaming also means we are less likely to be tempted to sacrifice long term gains for short term expediency at another's expense. Also, it is easier to resolve the inevitable conflicts within an overall mood of mutual commitment Finally, the benefit from "something you value may cost me nothing to help you achieve it" and vice versa, this is the icing on the cake of bioteam symbiosis.

Connectivity Zone: Rule 6 - Nurture the Network

- ✔ Bioteam connectivity ensures the team has good internal and external networks.
- ✔ Network connectivity is more important than network size.

Biologists have studied robustness in biological cells [22] by putting them into extreme conditions and seeing how they fail.

The conclusion is that biological fault tolerance depends on having a highly connected network.

However, it's not just any kind of highly connected network but one with a unique pattern of connectivity – the clustered or scale-free network. For example, in the case of *C. elegans*, a one-millimeter long worm with a mere 302 neurons, neighboring neurons are five times more likely to be linked than if the network was random – this is what it means to be a clustered network.

Research into nervous systems such as *C. elegans* shows that intelligence does not just depend on the number of neurons but more importantly the number of internal interconnections between them.

A key aspect of clustered networks are nodes that have many more connections than the average node, which are called hubs or connectors. Hubs play crucial roles in nature. For example, food chains are always dependent on "keystone species." You can remove other species with limited overall impact, but if you remove a keystone species the food chain will rapidly disintegrate.

Is it a case of 'the more connectivity the better' in a biological network?

Counter-intuitively the answer is NO. There is an optimum level in living systems known as "the edge of chaos," the point between order and chaos where living systems exist.

Too much order and "the islands of activity would be too small and isolated for complex behavior to propagate across the system." Too much chaos and "the system would be too sensitive to small perturbations to maintain its organization." [23]

A network with too many links becomes frozen (like ice) into rigidity and over-complexity. A network with too few links (like steam) lacks the necessary connections to make anything happen at all. So good networks are like liquids, existing in the "sweet spot" between solids and gases.

In a nutshell, network connectivity provides nature with robustness, fault tolerance and nervous system intelligence.

The power of weak ties

Social Network Analysis research [24] identifies two basic types of relationship, Weak and Strong Ties. This fits exactly with the biological concepts of clustered networks and Hub nodes.

Organizational teams tend to be biased towards one form of tie or the other. Teams seldom manage both types of ties well.

Strong ties are very good for getting work done, usually in small tightly bound groups. But, such teams are not generally known for their skills at listening and responding to signals from, and the changes in their external or customer environments.

Weak ties (hubs or connectors) are very good for listening, but not great for getting things actually done.

Good teams need both strong and weak ties

So, first, teams need to map out their networks and identify gaps. This can be done informally or using social network analysis software that generates network maps from interviews, or automatically from email or phone records.

Second, the team needs to create and nurture the right network to support both objectives, getting the job done right (strong ties) and getting the right job done (weak ties).

Third, organizational teams need to have the right hubs.

When the social network analysis is done it often reveals that only one person in a team holds many vital relationships. What happens if they get sick or overloaded, where is the fault tolerance? Also sometimes these people are not the best ones to be holding these relationships, they just happened by accident rather than design!

Hubs are also vital for ensuring the team gets "team intelligence" early enough to use it (See Rule 2 in the Leadership Zone).

Customer Hubs are very important but many teams neglect other equally critical hubs such as:

- Technical Hubs (who can get the IT department to do you favors)
- Social Hubs (who know the team's temperament)
- Organizational Hubs (who are very well connected to the company grapevine at a high level)

Some of the developments in "social software," for networking and business development could be particularly helpful here, if we rigorously applied them to our organizational teams as well as our personal networks. So bioteam network connectivity provides a team with:

- Responsiveness to changes in the external environment or market.
- Unofficial fast channels for getting help easier and quicker to avert a team or project crisis.
- "Jungle guides" who can help the team stay on the winding road to project success.

11. The Bioteams Execution Zone

- ✔ Act, Cooperate and Learn fast
- ✔ Learn how to swarm as a team, cooperate effectively as individuals and use fast iterative delivery cycles

Execution Zone: Rule 7 – Swarm!

- ✔ Bioteams develop consistent autonomous team member behavior

Nature's Way

Craig Reynolds, [25] a computer graphics researcher studied how bird flocks fly in formation to see whether there were simple rules that could be simulated in computer software.

As a group activity, "flocking" is extremely complex. However, it turns out that the underlying individual member behaviors that produce it are very simple. This must be the case, otherwise the individual birds, with their "bird brains," would not be able to follow the rules to the necessary consistency, while performing high speed flight maneuvers in close formation.

"Boids"

Reynolds came up with a virtual programmable bird called a "birdoid," which quickly and appropriately got shortened to "boid."

These computerized boids could be made to fly successfully in complex formation in 3-dimensional space provided the individual birds were programmed to consistently follow just three very simple rules:

1. *Separation:* steer to avoid crowding other local flock-mates.
2. *Alignment*: steer towards the average heading of the local flock-mates.
3. *Cohesion:* steer to move toward the average position of local flock-mates.

Other research [26] has also established that the complex behavior of nature's other groups such as ants, turtles, geese and termites can also be explained in the same way through sets of very simple individual member rules.

So in nature very simple individual member actions, so simple they can be easily followed without error, produce very sophisticated group behavior (without the members even being aware of the complex capabilities they are enabling).

Benefits of Rule to Nature

Nature's bioteam members don't have big brains or long memories. However their survival and positioning in the food chain depends on their ability to produce more sophisticated and more intelligent responses as a collective, than they could manage as individuals.

Their simple rule-based approach allows them to react exceptionally quickly to situations because the skills they need at an individual level are totally "present," and ready to use, without any thinking or preparation being required.

In human terms they are able to exhibit what educators would describe as "unconscious competence," the basis of true expert behavior – you don't think about what you do, you just do it.

Application of Rule to Organizational Teams

Today's common wisdom on creating high performance teams is that you need to create a team environment where the individual members can fully exercise their creativity and innovation.

This is very true, but I believe that nature's teams show us that it is only half the story of high performing teams. When we use the normal approach to high performing teams, we are actually jumping to the higher team capability level of "complex individual behavior," but skipping out the lower team capability level of "simple but highly consistent individual behavior."

In so doing, we sacrifice a number of important benefits because nature's examples prove that "coordinated individual simple behavior can produce more intelligent collective responses than un-coordinated individual complex behavior."

Now, obviously human teams are not going to gain much benefit from the kind of rules that ants or geese use. Human team members have the gift of human intelligence so we need to construct rules that are more abstract and allow space for team members to apply their own judgments.

O-R-G-A-N-I-C team member behaviors

I would suggest the following seven behavior rules as a good starting point for developing consistent autonomous member behavior in your teams:

- *Outgoing* – get to know all your team colleagues
- *Recruit* – look out for new external partners to strengthen the team's network
- *Go!* – network widely outside the team
- *Ask* – constantly ask for, and offer help to other team members
- *Note* – keep aware/abreast of issues of "team intelligence"
- *Investigate* – when you see something interesting, investigate it for the team
- *Collaborate* – join at least one team workgroup as an active member, don't just be a "reviewer"

3-Dimensional Team Members

These seven behaviors are designed to ensure that team members are "3-dimensional" in their operation, just like nature's teams, with the ability to concurrently listen, communicate and act in the following 3 dimensions:

1. Member-Member
2. Member-External (i.e., Customers, Partners and Competitors)
3. Member-Colony (i.e., Host Organizations and Teams)

Benefits of Rule to Organizational Teams

Nurturing consistent autonomous team member behavior provides distributed intelligence in our teams that will result in:

- Reduced coordination overheads
- Better fault tolerance – the ability to continue even when a particular part of the team is out of order
- Increased speed of spotting problems and opportunities

Execution Zone: Rule 8 – Tit for Tat

✔ Bioteam members use natural, personal, cooperation strategies.

Nature's Way

Research has discovered that many species in nature use a surprising strategy for cooperation known as TIT FOR TAT (TFT). The rules of TFT are very simple:

- Never be the first to defect
- Retaliate only after your partner has defected
- Be prepared to forgive after carrying out just one act of retaliation

It appears this strategy is highly popular in nature even in situations where the individuals are only able to recognize their species, rather than specific individuals.

Sticklebacks play TIT FOR TAT

One of the best empirical tests of TFT in nature is Milinski's laboratory experiments with stickleback fish in 1987. [21]

During the early stages of an attack by a stalking pike, some sticklebacks may leave their shoal to approach the predator, for a "predator inspection visit." They do this as a small group so that they can get very close and if the pike turns on them the fact they are in a group is confusing to it and increases all their chances of escape.

Milinski gave sticklebacks the chance to alter their behavior according to that of an imaginary companion fish, their reflection in a mirror. The mirror could be angled to give the illusion of a companion keeping up (cooperating) or lagging behind (defecting). In the experiment, the stickleback followed the rules of TFT exactly. For example, those fish with cooperating mirrors went closer to the predator and stayed there longer than the fish with defecting mirrors. Also the fish would usually forgive their cowardly companions up to a point and approach the predator again and again.

Some weaknesses in TFT

More recent research [27] has revealed some weaknesses in TFT, the biggest of which is that it the two players can become locked into a spiral of retaliation. The problem is, this can happen by accident such as errors in communication or interpretation but it may be impossible to break out of the retaliation cycle once it starts. Consequently another strategy WIN STAY–LOSE SHIFT (WSLS) ("if it's working keep doing it, if it's not change it") may be better in certain situations such as those with error-prone communications environments.

Benefits of Rule to Nature

TIT FOR TAT (and other biologically-based strategies such as WIN STAY-LOSE SHIFT) provides the most effective long-term cooperation strategies for many species in nature. In the longer term, cooperation is better for the whole community but is open to abuse by individual opportunists.

TFT allows for cooperation to be achieved but not at the expense of being exploited. This is achieved through TFT's retaliation and forgiveness responses that enable conflicting parties to then recover the cooperation after a breakdown.

Application of Rule to Organizational Teams

Recent research has shown that TIT FOR TAT is also the best long-term strategy for human cooperation [28]. Human teams and their members often say that they are committed to "playing Win-Win," which sounds great!

But what does it actually mean?

I propose that the best strategy for achieving Win-Win is not Win-Win, but, in fact, TIT FOR TAT!

Team members who say they are playing 'win-win' are generally referring to one of two very different personal collaboration strategies:

- *Mr. Nice Guy.* "I will assume you are cooperating with me until it is proven you are not. Then I won't work with you again." In this situation you can be easily taken advantage of, at that point you are often too resentful to try and put it right. Relationships that start in this kind of naivety generally end in tears!
- *Mr. Stand-off.* "I will assume you are not cooperating until it is proven you are, and if it is not conclusively proven after a certain time I will assume (privately) you are not a good partner." Relationships that start in this kind of distrust usually become self-fulfilling prophecies. So, start cautiously and you

won't be disappointed!

Win-Win is a state, not a strategy

So Win-Win is actually a highly desirable outcome/state, but is itself not the best strategy for getting there because Win-Win (in both forms above) has no means of challenging a non-cooperating partner and then recovering.

Team members need practical, personal collaboration strategies such as TFT, based on the three simple principles:

1. Never be the first to defect
2. Retaliate only after your partner has defected
3. Be prepared to forgive after carrying out just one act of retaliation

The other key point is to make it clear to all your team members that these are the rules you go by – secret TFT does not work!

This biological research has also shown [27] that a "cluster" of TFT players will grow and eventually convert other non-cooperative players to TFT.

However, it also shows that if more than three quarters of a population are using non-cooperative strategies then the team is beyond cooperation and is destined to stay in destructive behavior and its consequences.

Benefits of Rule to Organizational Teams

Viable, natural, personal cooperation strategies such as TIT FOR TAT keep the team together long enough to create the environment for a Win-Win state to emerge in the team.

Absence of such strategies creates distrust that results in a huge amount of waste, such as:

- People checking up on each other
- Team members falling out
- People playing politics
- Members raising personality issues with the leader rather than the offending person
- Email wars
- Team cliques

Consistent use of TFT in a bioteam by its members can avoid all this.

Execution Zone: Rule 9 – Team-based Genetic Algorithm

- ✔ Bioteams learn through experimentation, mutation and team learning sessions.

Nature's Way

Nature's teams solve problems using a trial and error process called genetic algorithms.

In the world of computing, a genetic algorithm is a technique for solving problems based on evolutionary techniques. It is so called because the required solutions to the problem are represented as genomes, as in DNA.

The genetic algorithm automatically creates a population of new solutions derived from this genome by random mutation. Various selection criteria are applied to pick the best solutions that are then "mated" to create a new batch.

The process then continues for thousands of cycles until the optimum solutions are eventually produced. In essence, a genetic algorithm works like this:

1. Breed new potential solutions
2. Evaluate how effective they are and pick the best ones
3. Breed new solutions from the best ones
4. Continue this way until the solution is optimum

But normal evolution is too slow

The big problem with genetic algorithms in nature is that progress only happens when a new generation is born. To put it simply, "no giraffe can increase the length of its own neck, only its children's."

Thus normal evolution proceeds only at the pace of generations, which is far too slow to be useful to human bioteams. However, nature's most intelligent living systems have found a way to achieve accelerated evolution through "intergenerational learning."

The main prerequisite for intergenerational learning is language. Language can enable group learning (it's necessary, but not sufficient for this) through "social propagation."

The second pre-requisite is that the species must use its language in stable groups, e.g., flocks.

Songbirds – an example of accelerated evolution

In the 1950s, British Bluetits as a species mastered the ability to peck open milk bottle tops that the milk men were delivering to the doorsteps of homes in the UK [29]. However, the British Robin never mastered this skill as a species even though they had the same degree of intelligence and language as the Bluetits.

Robins were every bit as innovative and mobile as Bluetits, and individual Robins could indeed peck open milk-tops. However, robins are territorial birds and do not flock and did not pass on this skill to their community.

Bluetits, however, move around in flocks of 8-10 birds and operating in this way were able to transfer the learning through entire the species via Social Propagation.

Benefits of Rule to Nature

This team-based genetic algorithm provides massive benefits to species that have it. They can achieve intergenerational learning, and therefore adapt much quicker than species who are constrained to develop at evolution's normal speed.

It allows them to achieve innovation that provides their species with more options for competition and survival. Effectively, they can choose how they compete within their food chains, and whether they are the predator or the prey.

Application of Rule to Organizational Teams

Our teams generally take a totally different approach to developing solutions and learning than the approach used in nature.

Our normal approach is *Ready-Aim-Fire,* whereas, nature is really *Fire-Aim-Ready.*

Nature's approach will seem counter-intuitive to us and the chasm between our current practice and nature might seem to be too vast to cross! For a real organizational example, see the story of Capital One summarized in chapter 6. [3]

Implementing Team-based Genetic Algorithms

To implement team-based genetic algorithms, we need to be

able to:

- Create a rich variety of potential solutions to a problem
- Test the best of these without major risk or cost
- Discuss the results as a team
- Refine the best ideas and try again

For this approach to be effective, we need to create a culture where individual failures are seen as essential building blocks for eventual success, and rather than being covered up, should be explored for learning and improvement.

The diagram below outlines a simple process, "Get-me," that a bioteam can use to facilitate rapid learning using the biological method:

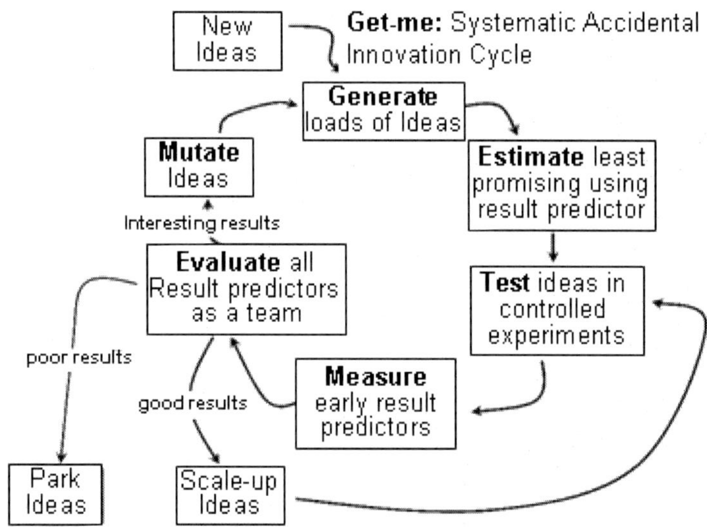

Benefits of Rule to Organizational Teams

The benefits of a Team-based biological approach to learning are huge and include:

- Development of rapid innovation and problem solving capabilities.
- Ability to produce breakthrough solutions from unexpected quarters.

- Early feedback from customers.
- Avoidance of costly failures by spotting them before they happen.
- Accelerated Learning as a team.
- Creating an exceptional staff development environment.

12. The Bioteams Organization Zone

- ✔ Self-organize for sustainability.
- ✔ Define the team as a change agent with a porous boundary, and a natural growth plan.

Organization Zone: Rule 10 – Autopoiesis (self-organization)

- ✔ Bioteams define themselves in terms of network transformations, not outputs.

Nature's Way

In their ground-breaking book, *The Tree of Knowledge: The Biological Roots of Human Understanding,* [30] Drs. Humberto Maturana and Francisco Varela, two Chilean biologist/neuroscientists, suggest a simple but profound model known as Autopoiesis, which is introduced using the simple little graphic below, to capture the very essence of living systems.

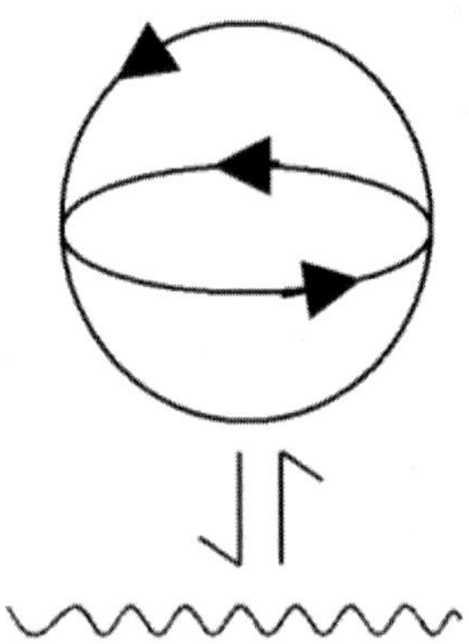

This model covers the complete spectrum of living systems, from the smallest organisms and animals through to communities, such as social insects right through to advanced human societies. Let us look at the three main "cornerstones" of the model of "living systems:"

1. The Self-Organizing Network

"What is distinctive about living systems, however, is that their organization is such that their only product is themselves, with no separation between the producer and the product. The being and doing of a living system are inseparable, and this is their specific mode of organization." [30, pp. 48-49]

The outer ring represents two interdependent ideas: the circle represents the boundary of the living system, and the arrow represents the processes and activities that operate within this boundary.

The boundary and the processes form a unity, you cannot have one without the other. The processes create the boundary, and the boundary provides a space in which the processes can operate.

In simple terms, the boundary demarks "the being" of the living system and the processes constitute "the doing." Each healthy living system is totally self-sustaining and produces everything it needs, provided the necessary food enters in through the boundary.

2. The Nervous System

The inner circle represents the nervous system, which is defined as "the system that couples the sensory and motor surfaces of the living system through a network of neurons whose patterns can be quite varied." [30]

Thus, the nervous system is a network of connections that enables the living system to respond, through movement and other internal processes, to triggers in its external environment.

The nervous system is important because it allows the development of language and self-consciousness within the living system. The more sophisticated the nervous system is, the more external triggers it can respond to, the more internal states it can sustain, and the wider its vocabulary of communications with its external environment.

3. The Communications System

The two half arrows outside the circles represent all forms of communications between the living system and its external environment. This external environment consists of other living systems and non-living stimuli (e.g., heat, sound, light, chemicals), but living systems don't differentiate on this basis.

Living systems do not "think" in terms of external entities, they only react through the nervous system, to the triggers they are sensitized to receive.

Where two living systems begin to communicate in a recurrent way, they are said to be coupled. In this case two things can happen: one can swallow up the other and they become one ("symbiosis"), or they can start to co-evolve together as a higher level system within which their individual separate identities are still maintained.

Benefits of Rule to Nature

The self-organizing network is absolutely fundamental to nature. It is this characteristic that makes the difference between a living and a non-living system.

If something does not have a self-organizing network it is not sustainable, it is either "not living" or in the process of dying. For example, an on-going scientific debate is whether viruses are alive or not. According to Maturana, viruses are not truly alive as they are not self-organizing networks.

"Viruses must have a host cell to live and reproduce. Outside of the host cell, viruses are pieces of genetic molecules that can do nothing by themselves. Viruses are right on the border between living and nonliving." [31]

Application of Rule to Organizational Teams

Thus according to this model a key aspect of any living system is that the function of each component is to produce or transform other components in the network.

What does this mean for a team?

Teams traditionally define their goals and roles in terms of activities, tasks or outputs. If a team wish to base themselves on nature's teaming principles they should instead define themselves in terms of the transformations they wish to make on their network components. This network includes all the teams members and partners, internal and external, individuals and organizations. This leads us to the fundamental cycle of transactions that keeps a bioteam alive:

- Step 1. Bioteam members produce and transform "customers."
- Step 2. These customers are prepared to commit projects, resources and support to the bioteam.
- Step 3. These resources feed and energize the team's metabolism to subsequently produce and transform more customers (Step 1) ... and so it becomes a self-sustaining network.

How do the members of a bioteam produce or transform the other network components?

They interact with them either directly (e.g., recruiting a new member), or indirectly through the following types of transformation:

1. Helping them build more valuable relationships with each other.
1. Helping them acquire new practices and skills for working together.
2. Building new infrastructures (e.g., a collaboration web-site) to help them work together.
3. Assisting them to create new intellectual property, which increases their collective value to customers.

Biological processes often require a catalyst (or enzyme) to be present, to enable and accelerate the required chemical transformations – the same applies in organizational teams.

Examples of important organizational catalysts include "brokers" (to identify prospective customers) and "coaches" (to help the team get better at working together).

The key point here is that each bioteam goal, and role, should be primarily defined in terms of what other living network components it transforms, not in terms of inanimate outputs.

For example, a broker might produce prospective customers and transform them into committed customers. A founding team member might produce prospective members and in partnership with other members transform them into committed members.

Collectively these set of role interactions must create a positive feedback loop around the team's customers, for the team to be viable and exhibit the necessary circularity between the teams roles. In other words, the total set of interactions between the roles should create a "closed system" that provides re-enforcing feedback loops to sustain it.

Benefits of Rule to Organizational Teams

This approach can yield huge benefits to an organizational team:

- It puts the team's focus on making positive impacts on key people and enterprises rather than producing things.
- It brings relationships and collaboration right into the center of the team.
- It creates virtuous cycles with positive re-enforcing feedback loops (e.g., as described in *Tit for Tat* (Rule 8) in the Execution Zone, how small group of effective win-win players can convert a whole team to this style of cooperation over time).

Organization Zone: Rule 11 – Porous Membranes

✔ Bioteam boundaries are open to energy but closed to waste.

Nature's Way

As I mentioned in the previous rule, a very important aspect of living systems is the boundary between them and their external environment. Biological research shows that these boundaries are very special in that they are both open and closed at the same time.

One of the best examples of these living boundaries is in the biological cell, a universal feature of all cellular life is a living cell boundary known as the "cell membrane."

Frijof Capra writes, [32] "A membrane is very different from a cell wall. Whereas cell walls are rigid structures, membranes are always active, opening and closing continually, keeping certain substances out and letting others in." This membrane thus acts as a semi-permeable barrier around the cell, that:

- Maintains the delicate chemical balance of the cell to allow its metabolism to function effectively.
- Provides an exit for excessive calcium waste to be pumped out.
- Protects the cell from harmful environmental influences.
- Creates a safe space that defines the identity of the cell.

Benefits of Rule to Nature

Cellular membranes provide three major benefits to the cell:

1. *Good stuff gets in.* Membranes allow energy, food, useful chemicals and helpful micro-cellular life (symbionts) to come in.
2. *Bad stuff stays out.* Membranes ensure harmful chemicals (poisons), and destructive micro-cellular life (parasites and pests) are kept out.
3. *Waste gets put out.* Membranes provide a channel for the removal of the cell's waste products and dead components that, if not removed, would soon poison the cell.

Application of Rule to Organizational Teams

How can we apply the concept of the biological membrane to our teams?

Good stuff gets in

A bioteam should be constantly open throughout its life, to new members joining. Bioteams have a large set of part-time members, supporters and friends – they don't just run on core and full-time members. Bioteams have members who are external to the main organization including suppliers and customers.

A key responsibility of the leaders and senior members of a bioteam is to constantly look for new talent who may be useful in some capacity for the team.

Instead of "sealing" our teams at the early stage of a project we should instead be constantly seeking to grow the team network throughout the life of the project as the need and opportunity arises.

Bad stuff stays out

There are two types of bad stuff in teams – pests and parasites!

A pest is somebody who intends to achieve his/her goals at the expense of the rest of the team, no matter what the cost. Typical pest behavior is using information gained through the team to one's own personal gain even if it damages the team. Pests should be avoided at all costs, however, they can be hard to detect, as they are usually secretive or you would not have them on the team in the first place

A parasite is somebody who is in the team purely to satisfy his/her own goals, they don't care either way what impact this has on the team. Parasites will usually stop short of actions that would destroy the team, as they need the team to exist if they are to keep feeding off it.

Typical parasite behavior is doing as little work as possible but still trying to share the full rewards of any team success. Parasites are as destructive as pests and even more difficult to spot because their behavior is more subtle.

Parasites embody 'freeloading behavior' that results in other team members becoming over-worked, becoming resentful, demotivated and even leaving the team (if not physically, then emotionally/mentally).

In a nutshell the difference between pests and parasites is that parasites need the team to survive but pests do not!

- *The first barrier to pests and parasites is the team selection process.* A bioteam can avoid 'bad eggs' by ensuring that the other founding team members' views are respected in the choice of team members. The key thing to look out for here, is a mismatch on values and motives. Problems with competencies can generally be corrected, while problems on values are very difficult to resolve.
- *The second barrier to pests and parasites is team ground rules.* Team Ground Rules capture succinctly the non-negotiable membership behavior rules, for being a "good standing member" of the team.

One of the best ways to define the ground rules is by asking the whole team a series of questions such as:

- What behavior by another member would make you no longer wish to be part of this team?
- What behavior is forgivable and what is not?
- What rules do you wish to have around the balancing of information transparency versus reasonable privacy?
- How to you wish to resolve issues (about the project) and conflicts (between team members)?

The best way to do this is not a group discussion but to get the individual team member responses uninfluenced by the other members, aggregate them and then discuss as a group the points of agreement and the points of difference.

The team members should also define the "sanctions system," that they will apply (and be subject to) when team members fail to honor the ground rules. These sanctions should start informally and progress gradually, e.g., a quiet word, a verbal warning, a written warning, and so on.

Benefits of Rule to Organizational Teams

Adopting the biological membrane approach in an organizational team can provides two major benefits:

1. The "continuously open" team approach ensures a wide team, with access to the required talent, influence and grapevine networks.
2. The use of "ground rules" ensures that members are productive, and avoids both team pests and parasites.

Organization Zone: Rule 12 – Emerge!

- ✔ Bioteams scale up in harmony with natural growth and decay cycles.

Nature's Way

Let's start by looking at the typical lifecycle of an Ant Colony – one of nature's most successful teams. While, Ant colonies vary greatly in their social structure, they all share four basic stages in their development and life that I have generalized in the diagram below:

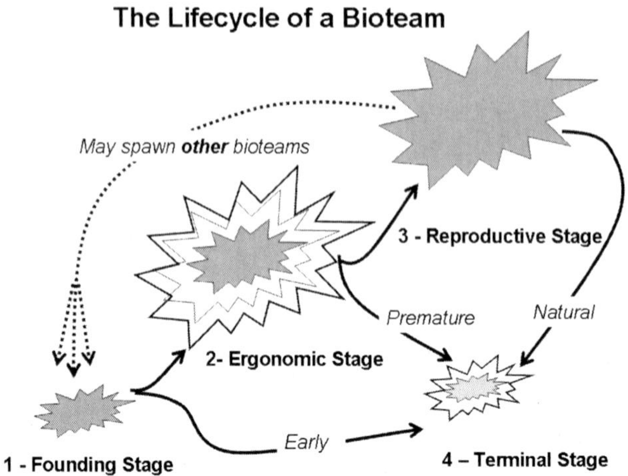

The Founding Stage

The first stage is the founding stage, in which a young virgin ant queen leaves the nest of her mother and flies until she has met and been inseminated by a few males. The males soon die without returning to their nests. Then the female finds a suitable place in the soil or in a rotting tree to build her nest. She forages and cares for her first brood until they are adults.

In the ant world there is a fascinating "bootstrap scenario" in the founding stage, where the Queen must give birth to exactly the right blend of workers, who must quickly grow and find food to replenish her weakened state of energy, to allow her to continue giving birth and begin populating the rest of the colony. If she gets this even slightly wrong then the colony simply dies.

The other main risk at this stage is the choice of nesting location, it needs to work in terms of both protection from predators, and proximity to food sources.

Mortality rate for queens (and their colonies) at this stage exceeds 99%! [33]

The Ergonomic Stage

Next the colony enters the second stage, known as the ergonomic stage. Now the queen devotes herself to egg-laying while the workers forage, care for the young, protect the queen and enlarge the nest. This stage, which centers on colony growth, lasts for a period ranging from four months to five years, depending on the species of ant.

In the ergonomic stage the main focus is to quickly get big enough to avoid being easy prey for enemies and to stake a position with the neighboring ant colonies who will be utterly ruthless in trying to destroy a young colony as they represent competition for food and other resources.

The ergonomic phase is about getting the team to a viable critical mass and blend of castes as quickly as possible.

If a colony can make it through to the two-year mark, then its mortality rate drops to about 5%! [33]

The Reproductive Stage

When the colony reaches a suitable size, it can enter the reproductive stage. Now new queens and males are produced that, at the right moment, leave the nest to produce new colonies, beginning the founding cycle all over again. Typically, after about five years colony size starts to stabilize. The colonies become as big as they are going to grow, and they then enter the reproductive stage.

Once a colony reaches this stage, it has a 95% chance of staying that size and surviving for the next 10 - 15 years.[33]

The Terminal Stage (i.e., Death!)

Why does a colony die? Natural or man-made disaster aside, the primary cause of colony death is the death of the queen. More precisely the ending of the queens ability to produce offspring. Typically a queen, and thus her colony, can live for about 20 years.

Some species of ants, such as Pharaohs ants that occupy an ecological niche, produce multiple queens and can thus effectively live forever. However there is a cost! Such immortality leads to in-breeding, which leaves the species less able to adapt to the environment.

Death of the colony is therefore part of the process – as Edward O. Wilson says "for most kinds of ants, old colonies die so that new colonies can be safely born." [18]

Benefits of Rule to Nature

Again the benefits of this rule to nature are absolutely fundamental. The process by which living things come into existence, grow and survive is very high risk, with critical vulnerabilities in the early stages that must be catered for.

It needs time to be nurtured and all of this must take place in a dangerous, unpredictable and extremely hostile environment.

The natural lifecycle outlined here is nature's optimum solution that has evolved over millions of years as the best way for living things to grow. We disregard it at our peril!

Application of Rule to Organizational Teams

This biological model is quite different from the normal linear models of team development maturity we are used to.

Traditional team development models that show teams nicely progressing, always forward and upward, from one well defined stage to the next do not reflect nature, or real organizational life.

Any change in management approach to incubating bioteams, therefore, needs to start with a realistic lifecycle!

Let's apply the four stages to organizational teams.

The Founding Stage

Just like the ant colony, this is the stage where a team makes choices that cannot be easily reversed.

If the founding leader (or leaders) does not pull the right people around him/her to bootstrap the team, then it will fail, too.

Similarly, poor choice of the location for nesting in ant colonies equates to the organizational team leaders badly choosing, designing and shaping the teams' initial aims and objectives. It is the shaping of these objectives that will motivate the team members and ensure realistic chances of success.

Note the 99% mortality rate, I think this same percentage also applies to organizational teams, but we often don't actually spot that the team died until much later when it fails to deliver. Sometimes, our teams are effectively dead right from the start of the project, but not buried till the end of it!

The Ergonomic Stage

The ergonomic stage is where the team gets "filled-out" into the right shape and scale for the task.

Like the ant colony, it is important to know the optimum size and blend of skills and roles, to enable the team to achieve its purpose. If the team operates below this level then it will not achieve peak performance.

Good role definition that enables effective division of labor is critical at this stage. Division of labor requires team members to be able to do different things at the same time.

The Reproductive Stage

When an ant colony reaches a suitable size, it can enter the reproductive stage.

In organizational teams this should be when the team objective is secure, and there exists an opportunity to seed other teams with the learning, to avoid staleness and enable organizational, rather than just individual, learning.

Unlike an ant colony, human bioteam members can exist in multiple bioteams (even simultaneously), which creates an important opportunity for us to "reproduce" and join new teams before our current team dies.

A good strategy is to have the stronger bioteam members play coaching and advisory roles to newly forming teams.

The Terminal Stage (i.e., Death!)

Organizational teams like nature's teams cannot be immortal. There must also be an end, otherwise the members become stale and cease to function effectively.

So an organizational team needs a way to recycle members out and bring new members in on a regular basis. As well as addressing the problems of staleness, this is also crucial in terms of organizational learning.

Arie De Geuss, [29] writing in his book, *The Living Company,* suggests that job rotation is absolutely critical for organizational learning – otherwise you just have individual learning.

Benefits of Rule to Organizational Teams

First, the natural lifecycle allows you to find out where you are and plan accordingly.

If you are setting up a new bioteam, then you have the luxury of starting at the founding stage and can take care of all the prerequisite steps.

If your team already exists you may be fully operational (e.g., in the ergonomic stage), but with some key foundations missing (e.g., Ground Rules), to be an effective bioteam.

It is important to make a realistic assessment of where you are, what the gaps are, and what needs to be put in place before trying to move forward.

If you don't do this, the team will not reach its potential in the ergonomic phase, and certainly will never reach the reproductive stage, where the team members have the experience and ability to reproduce by "founding" other successful bioteams, within or outside your organization.

Second, the natural lifecycle allows you to design a realistic strategy for change management in the team.

The biological team lifecycle should remind us that the team is not just a collection of its members, but a living thing in itself and must be encouraged and nudged towards more advanced states, rather than simply being wound up like a clock!

Change in living systems cannot be "managed." Living system can only be perturbed, so we should not think so much in terms of change management but more in terms of perturbation management.

Ecologists recognize two types of change in ecosystems and social systems: [34]

- Type 1 – Progressive change due to internal self-organizing processes.
- Type 2 – Quantum change from one "stability domain" to another because of external disturbances.

A key leadership role in a bioteam is to act as a catalyst to help it "jump" its operation and performance to a higher level stability domain through Type 2 change.

Part 3: The Mechanisms of Bioteaming

13. Pheromone-style communications

Introduction to Pheromone Signaling

Pheromone-based messaging is the oldest and most evolved form of biological signaling, using chemicals to communicate through smell and taste.

Today's virtual teams and mobile groups can use it to significantly improve the way they use email, messaging and presence-aware technologies.

When you mention the word Pheromone at a dinner party the most likely association you will register is about strange perfumes you can buy that make you irresistible to the opposite sex.

For example, books like *The Scent of Eros: Mysteries of Odor in Human Sexuality* [35] extol the wonders of Human Pheromones.

However human sexual attraction is just one small aspect of what Pheromones are about, as the sense of smell is the oldest of the natural senses, the most evolved and the basis of most biological signaling systems.

Pheromone messaging is used by almost every animal or insect, large or small, on land, air or water dwelling. For example, if you walk round the wonderful Dinosaur exhibit at The Natural History Museum in London, you will learn that it is believed that dinosaurs had an amazing sense of smell that they used in hunting their prey. In terms of brain size, comparing the part of the brain associated with smell in a Tyrannosaurus Rex, with our human brains is like comparing an orange to a pea!

13 Characteristics of Pheromone Signaling

Pheromone messaging uses chemicals to effect communications between animals and insects, through smell and taste and have the following characteristics (for more details see *Pheromones and Animal Behavior – Communication by smell and taste* [36]):

1. Broadcast and Individual
2. 1-way
3. Whole species
4. Simple vocabulary
5. Intraspecies and Interspecies
6. Robust Delivery
7. Low energy
8. Longevity potential
9. Message Range
10. Multichannel
11. Quick and Slow Responses
12. Anonymity of sender
13. Location Information

We will look at each characteristic in turn, and consider the practical ways groups and teams currently could reorganize their electronic communications along bioteaming principles:

1. Broadcast and Individual: Pheromones are predominantly broadcasts to many, but can also be used between individuals in a species.

Practical Application: Within a trusted group we can be more transparent by broadcasting to the whole group (one-to-many) or communicating with a single individual (one-to-one). In a later chapter, "Three Communication patterns in bioteams," I explore the benefits of reviewing and reducing "one-to-some" communications.

2. 1-way: Messages are not replied to.

Practical Application: Use of 2-way messaging can seriously slow a team down as all replies are waited for. Teams should use 1-way messaging as a default, and 2-way as an exception.

3. Whole species: Pheromone messaging is available to all the members of the species, however, different castes within a species may have different messages they send and "listen for."

Practical Application: All members of the group should have full and equal messaging rights, including the ability to communicate with the entire group. This is often restricted due to concerns around spamming and misuse. A new mindset is required here. If, whole group messaging is abused there are ways to correct it, such as using reputation management systems, where the *spamming user loses digital reputation.*

4. Simple vocabulary: The messages are simple stimulus-response templates and contain no complex body information.

Practical Application: You should try to put the essence of the message into small number of characters (100-200), or even to use a set of abbreviated message types, e.g., Feedback, Vote, Opportunity. This enables the messages to be acted on only by reading the message header, and is also convenient for sending by SMS and IM. We spend far too much time on message bodies and, even worse, attachments that our co-workers often do not read or simply skim – especially if they are on mobile devices.

5. Intraspecies and Interspecies: Pheromone messages are predominantly used within a species. However, they can be also used between species (deliberately or inadvertently). Interspecies messaging happens in two ways. Synomones are "honest" messages' where the message can be relied on, and is for the benefit of both sender and receiver. For example, an alarm message where two or more species share a common prey. Allomones are 'dishonest' messages where the sender is attempting to mislead the other species through some form of chemical propaganda. Messages can also be eavesdropped by other species (typically prey) that are known as Kairomones.

Practical Application: Can you organize your communications into multiple self-contained groups, with the ability to send and receive messages to/from other groups?

6. Robust Delivery: There are two main aspects to this. "Flow Round" – where messages can flow round an obstacle in their path (unlike visual messaging), and "Darkness Transmission" where the messages can be transmitted and received at night.

Practical Application: Can you create a multi-channel capability (e.g., email, IM and SMS) for your team communications, to ensure robust delivery of messages in remote and "noisy" environments?

7. Low energy: The main energy requirement in messaging is for the sender to generate the message. Because of the minuscule amounts of chemical compounds that need to be created, pheromones are much cheaper to send, than say, acoustic messages, such as a cricket chirruping. They are also very low in energy costs, to receive.

Practical Application: How can you make your messages as simple as possible to transmit? Even more importantly, making them easy to reply (minimum clicks), particularly for users on the move, using mobile devices.

8. Longevity potential: Unlike acoustic or visual messages, chemically-based pheromones have the potential for persistence, as the chemical can be available in the environment for an extended period.

Practical Application: Is there a place where all your group communications, for all your different channels, get stored, aggregated, archived and available to all users to inspect? The danger with a lot of short messages such as SMS or IM is that once sent they are lost, and are not integrated with the team's email and other communications.

9. Message Range: Pheromone messages have a natural range as the scent is stronger the closer the receiver is to the transmission point.

Practical Application: Are you using group rings and sub-groups to ensure you are not notifying team members unnecessarily? Most groups can be divided into a number of concentric rings – inner, middle and outer – each of which has different levels of engagement and notification requirements. For more on group and team rings see chapter: "The three rings of member commitment in a bioteam."

10. Multichannel: Pheromones can be used in conjunction with other messages for two main reasons. The first reason is redundancy, where over-communication via more than one channel is used to ensure the messages gets through. The second reason is, when the pheromone only contains part of the message and the other part is transmitted over another channel. To fully understand the message the receiver needs to read both channels.

Practical Application: Like point 6, Robust Delivery, you should be able to specify a number of channels for messages including email, SMS, and IM and to allow redundancy, if required, by having messages simultaneously transmitted over more than one channel.

11. Quick and Slow Responses: There are two types of pheromone messages – *Releaser messages* that release an immediate effect in the receiver and *Primer messages* that prime the receiver to commence a longer-term response, such as the production of sperm or to initiate caste transformation.

Practical Application: You need a way to indicate what type of message you have just sent, immediate action or not, and a 'reminder system' to ensure the longer-term messages are not forgotten about.

12. Anonymity of sender: If a pheromone message is broadcast rather than individually transmitted then it is not possible to identify the sender of a message. This has benefits (anonymity) and disadvantages (location of sender).

Practical Application: Anonymous message senders create all sorts of issues around authenticity and SPAM. I would not recommend it. However, you should allow the sender to be able to request anonymous replies where this is appropriate, such as a vote or a group feedback session. Anonymity of reply is needed where the question is such that identification of the replier would destroy their ability to offer an authentic reply, e.g., "Do you think I am leading this team into trouble?"

13. Location Information: Pheromone messaging can be used to lay trails and can therefore be used to convey location information – for example of a new food source or a prey.

Practical Application: It is definitely in the future as opposed to today but you could use location information in messages, such as find the nearest team member, via the growing capabilities of location-based services facilities within team member's mobile phones.

Chapter Summary

I have outlined 13 characteristics of pheromone messaging that represent the most evolved system of group signaling on the planet. Many of these characteristics can be included in the way we use electronic communications in teams and groups, by relatively simple changes in our behavior, and modest reconfiguration of our existing communication technologies.

14. Four unique ways bioteams get things done

Four habits of bioteams

From my work with emerging and established bioteams, I have noticed that there are four ways they seem to get work done that I don't recall seeing much in more conventional teams. I believe they are important differentiating characteristics of bioteams. So what are the four ways bioteams get work done?

1. One knows – all know! When one team member finds out something that MAY be important they make sure everyone else knows about it just in case. I referred to this earlier as Team Intelligence. Even if the information is not relevant to the member who obtains it, they are trained to think of the big picture and pass it on. Without this a team is flying blind without any early warning system of potential problems and opportunities. For more on this see Bioteams Rule 2.

2. Ask the network: Bioteams are not afraid to ask for help and take seriously, requests for help. This means that if I personally cannot help I wont stop there. I will pass your request to my network and manage the follow through, to ensure that if someone in my network can help, you will know about it. This is the sign of a really good team.

3. Co-invention: There are times where the entire team needs to contribute to a decision or other task, this is often referred to as The Wisdom of Crowds. [37] There are other times where the team needs to pick the right person or subgroup for a task, and just let them get on with it – this is Collective Intelligence.

If a team uses the Wisdom of Crowds where it should have used Collective Intelligence, or vice versa, they will just get into a mess. A bioteam knows when to use which type of team decision. Let me clarify.

The Wisdom of Crowds, as popularized by the book of the same name, is about applying the intelligence of a group to a certain kind of problem where majority rule, or averaging, is appropriate. For example, ask the audience in a TV quiz show or estimating the effort in building a software product (using, for example, the excellent Delphi Technique).

I would call this Averaging Group Intelligence rather than Collective Intelligence as you take into account multiple inputs in your calculation to attempt to find the best answer (the average or most popular).

Collective Intelligence, Group Intelligence or Team Intelligence is about finding the best answer a group can give to a problem, based on identifying the member in the group who should know best.

I accept that this is a simplified definition of "Collective Intelligence," as it can also be used in the sense of "Swarm Intelligence" to explain mass behavior of agents such as ants and bees, where an intelligence beyond the individual components emerges. We are not talking about that here.

For example, to devise the best sales strategy you should find and ask the person or persons who are best at sales strategy.

If there is more than one contender for expertise then you might consider asking the group which one they favor, a good Wisdom of Crowds question!

However, you definitely should not ask each group member and then try to find some kind of middle ground, or lowest common denominator that accommodates in some way, bits of all their responses.

Collective Intelligence is Exclusive Group Intelligence – finding and picking the best intelligence in the group, for a specific question.

Groupthink is Collective Intelligence gone wrong.

So in my opinion, the Wisdom of Crowds and Collective Intelligence are totally different and easily distinguished techniques.

In the Wisdom of Crowds you usually make a calculation, whereas, in Group Intelligence you usually make a choice. Each is appropriate to certain kinds of situations – but if you use the wrong one for the wrong situation you will get a bad result.

4. Leveraged Engagement: Good teams have both intra-team relationships (strong ties) and inter-team relationships (weak ties). These weak ties are not evenly spread, but tend to reside in a few team connectors (as popularized in Malcolm Gladwell's book, *The Tipping Point* [38]).

A smart team uses leveraged engagement when it needs outside help, i.e., they use their internal connectors and their collective relationships with important external connectors to get the help they need quickly. No team can survive without the ability to call in short-order favors from friends in the wider organization.

Chapter Summary

Bioteams:

1. Share information immediately if they think it might be useful to others.
2. Constantly ask their internal networks for help.
3. Co-invent with their full team at the right times and know when to use The Wisdom of Crowds and when to use Collective Intelligence.
4. Leverage external relationships when they need to engage with their external communities.

15. The six key processes in a bioteam

Natural Team Processes

In traditional organizational teams we have processes like selection, mobilization, planning, operations and dissolution.

Bioteams have a totally different set of natural processes: Foraging, Co-Evolution, Reproduction, Nurture, Maintenance and Metabolism.

If we wish to successfully emulate nature then we need to assess the degree to which these natural processes are present in our teams.

A bioteam is a self-organizing network

Fritjof Capra in his book, "The Hidden Connections," [32] defines the biological cell, which is also a self-organizing network, as follows: "We have learned that a cell is a membrane-bounded, self-generating, organizationally closed metabolic network; that it is materially and energetically open, using a constant flow of matter and energy to produce, repair and perpetuate itself; and that it operates far from equilibrium, where new structures and new forms of order may spontaneously emerge, thus leading to development and evolution."

From studying biological teams (such as the cell) and socio-biological teams (such as ants) [18], songbirds [29] and dolphins [39]), it is clear that these teams operate a small number of common processes that enable them to react very effectively with their environments and to take care of their internal members and structures.

These bioteam processes and the relationships between them are illustrated in the diagram below.

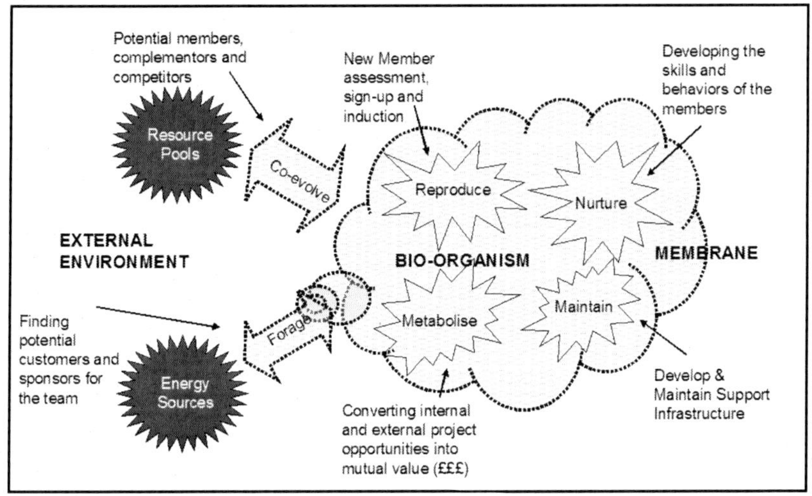

The first two bioteam processes focus on the team's external environment:

Process 1. Foraging: The Foraging Process is how the team engages with Energy Sources to provide food. In a human bioteam this translates to how the team engages with its prospective customers (at many levels), and sponsors who can generate "food" for the team through contracts, project briefs, funding and authorizations.

If a bioteam has an inadequate foraging process it will not obtain the kind of work and kind of support it will need to produce significant value.

Process 2. Co-Evolution: The second key externally focused bioteam process is the Co-Evolution process. The term co-evolution is used frequently to refer to the fact that a living system is impacted by, and impacts on its, external environment.

A simple example given by Maturana [30] is that our feet co-evolve with our shoes. Our shoes change our feet and our feet change our shoes.

I could also have called this process the "Co-opetition" process, after the book of the same name [40], which points out that businesses often have to cooperate to create value, and compete to capture it.

Even deadly enemies have to cooperate sometimes, an example is terrorist groups using agreed codes to ensure governments and police forces know they are not dealing with hoaxes.

Co-evolution is about how a human bioteam focuses on external resource pools (individuals and groups), and draws in talent, either in the form of team members or alliances.

A key element of this process is managing the tension between the teams and sometimes between other competitive groups or situations that might compete with the team for resources such as finance, potential members or senior management attention.

The other four bioteam processes focus on the teams internal mechanisms.

Process 3. Reproduction: Reproduction concerns how new members get signed up and successfully inducted into "operationally ready" team members. The reproduction process needs to be fed with a stream of prospective new members from the foraging process.

Most team leaders know that if they start with the wrong set of people in their team then they are probably doomed no matter how well they manage them.

Process 4. Nurture: Nurture is about developing the skills and behaviors of all levels and types of team members. This involves learning new practices around collaborative working, as well as skills that relate to the specific purpose of the bioteam (e.g., software development, marketing or Six Sigma). It also includes looking after team members from a relational point of view.

Process 5. Maintenance: Maintenance is about maintaining and developing the bioteam infrastructures (both virtual and physical), that the team will rely on.

Maintenance is similar to Nurture with the fundamental difference being that nurture looks after the members of the team whereas maintenance looks after the artifacts of the team.

One of the best examples of Maintenance in biological teams is Termites. Termites are considered to be the master architects of the animal world.

Mitchell Resnick [26] notes, " On the plains of Africa, termites construct giant, mound like nests rising more than ten feet tall, thousands of times taller than the termites themselves…Certain species of termites even use architectural tricks to regulate the temperature inside their nests, in effect turning their nests into elaborate air-conditioning systems."

We should not forget that, like ants, termites are totally self-managed.

Process 6. Metabolism: Metabolism is the last and the most important internal bioteam process. In the biological world, metabolism is about converting food into energy to fuel the organism's growth.

In a human bioteam, metabolism is about transforming good project opportunities identified through foraging, into undisputed value for their customers. This creates a virtuous feedback cycle, where energy is produced to sustain the team and its growth through money, resources and enhanced reputation.

This process is the "engine room" where the bioteam members, working collaboratively, create value or not!

Bioteam processes interlock: It is important to note that these bioteam processes are massively interdependent and should not be thought of in a siloed manner. Similarly the distinction of "external" versus "internal" process should not be overly stressed.

For example, an effective bioteam will co-evolve with customers engaged through foraging and serviced through metabolism.

Chapter Summary

Bioteams have a totally different set of processes than traditional teams:

1. Foraging
2. Co-Evolution
3. Reproduction
4. Nurture
5. Maintenance
6. Metabolism.

16. Three Communication patterns in bioteams

Nature's Team communication patterns

From studying nature's teams it seems there are three dominant patterns of communication that are used in a biological group.

All three patterns also have their place in the electronic communications we use in our human teams. However one of them, if over-used, can be destructive or indicate the absence of crucial group support structures. For simplicity, I call these three dominant patterns of communication:

- The Shout (one-to-many)
- The Whisper (one-to-one)
- The Gossip (one-to-some)

Shouting

Shouting involves communicating with the whole group.

This is the main pattern of communication used by the social insects. It is a 1-way broadcast communication, not requiring a reply. In nature it is achieved in the case of ants through scent trails (pheromones) and for bees via dances such as the waggle dance.

Human groups need to be able to do 2-way broadcasts, for example to schedule meetings, conduct polls or obtain feedback.

However, I would suggest that it is even more important for human groups to learn to use 1-way broadcasting much more. The current addiction to 2-way messaging is one of the ways a group gets slowed down unnecessarily.

Whispering

Whispering is a 1:1 private communication pattern.

This also happens frequently in nature, as ants and bees can communicate 1:1 by stroking each other or by exchanging fluids.

Human groups need to be able to whisper too. Not all conversations can be transparent, some are simply not relevant to the group and others are inappropriate.

A simple practical example of the need for whispering is on a web-conference, where you need to get the administrator's attention to say you wish to speak. Similarly, the administrator may need to get your attention to tell you discretely, you are talking to loudly, too quietly or too much.

Whispering is also a vital group "grooming" activity between team members where trust and rapport is built through regular 1:1 conversations.

Gossiping

This third pattern of communication, gossiping, which I define as a private communication to some but not all members of the group is the one we need to be very careful about.

Generally biological groups such as ants or bees do not use this form of communication.

Ad hoc and random gossiping can be quite harmless and entirely useful in a group. However, the danger arises when the gossiping recurrently involves the same subset of team members. An obvious risk is that a clique is being nurtured within the group that may, at some point, undermine the transparency and trust in a high performing team.

Alternatively, gossiping may indicate that you are missing a sub-group or a leadership ring. In the interests of transparency, these structures should be made explicit to all and not kept a secret.

For more on leadership rings, see the chapter, "The three rings of member commitment in a bioteam."

Chapter Summary

So, there are three main patterns of electronic communication within groups – shouting, gossiping and whispering.

We need to keep a note of how much each pattern is used in our teams, to ensure we use the right one at the right time, and be particularly careful about gossiping as it may point to cliques forming or missing structures.

17. The 4 Types of teamwork in a bioteam

What is "Teamwork?"

Although there are many different definitions, in nature the definition of "teamwork" is very precise. There are four different types of "teamwork" in biological teams: Solowork, Crowdwork, Groupwork and Teamwork itself.

A bioteam knows how and when to use all four forms – the choice depends on the specific task at hand.

When we talk about Teamwork, we generally mean different things. For some, a team is a group of people with a shared purpose. For others, a team must also have a deadline. For some others, a team must also embody some degree of cooperative working. If, we are really serious about improving teams and teamwork, then we need to get more rigorous about what we actually mean.

A Biological definition of "teamwork"

Carl Anderson and Nigel Franks [41] have undertaken unique research into insects, animal, human and even robot teams. They were interested in the degree to which these different groups are capable of exhibiting "teamwork." To do this, they developed a rigorous but practical way to assess whether particular group activities constitute "teamwork."

Teams undertake different kinds of tasks

If, instead of focusing on the team members we look instead at the tasks they undertake together, we find four types:

1. Individual Task
2. Group Task
3. Partitioned Task
4. Team Task

Individual Tasks

These can be completed by single individuals without help. I call it 'Solowork'. Solowork is an important aspect of organizational team behavior, sometimes, it's the best way to get things done.

Group Tasks

These tasks require multiple team members to do the same activity concurrently. For example, ants or soccer supporters conducting ritual symbolic displays in territorial battles with another groups. There is concurrency, but no division of labor. Different individuals must do the same things at the same time.

I call this "Crowdwork." Crowdwork has a place in organizational teams such as team review meetings, brainstorming and team social gatherings. However, Crowdwork can also be an indication of poor role definition and consequent misuse of resources. For example, a meeting where everyone starts to play the same role at the same time generally does not produce useful outcomes.

Partitioned Tasks

This is where a task is split into two or more subtasks that can be organized sequentially. For example, for a Bee, "Collect and Store Nectar" can be split into Sub-Task 1, "Collect Nectar" and Sub-Task 2, "Store Nectar." There is division of labor but no concurrency.

I call this 'Groupwork'. Lots of organizational teamwork can be achieved through Groupwork - it lends itself particularly well to asynchronous communication methods such as email and shared document areas.

Team Tasks

Requires multiple individuals to perform different tasks concurrently. Different individuals must do different things at the same time. There is both division of labor and concurrency.

This is real 'Teamwork" and requires the most complex coordination between team players. In biological teams "Teamwork" is used extensively for critical activities such as responding to a threat or exploiting an opportunity.

What blend of "teamwork" is your team?

Your should try to assess the different kinds of teamwork in your teams. For example, take a look at the way your team does Collaborative Document Development. One popular approach is that a single author develops the entire document, copies it to the other members and then decides what to do with all their review comments. This looks mostly like Solowork with a little bit of Groupwork at the end.

Another common approach is to break up the document into multiple independent sections, each with a different author. They are independently reviewed and edited. A single author is appointed to pull the document together via a management summary, and common formatting for the different sections. This is still pure Groupwork, but still not Teamwork.

A more Teamwork-oriented approach to this would be to allocate each team member certain horizontal responsibilities, that span document sections (*Teamwork*), plus some vertical responsibilities, for specific sections of the document (*Solowork*), plus some group review responsibilities.

You need all flavors of teamwork in your team. Each type of teamwork appropriate for certain tasks – a bioteam uses them all, and in the right context:

- *Solowork* is a valid and useful activity in teams – in certain situations, it is simply the most efficient way to get things done.
- *Groupwork* lends itself well to asynchronous communication methods.
- *Crowdwork* may point to poor team role definition that wastes team members time.

Teamwork (in the biological sense) seems to be relatively rare in organizational teams. It requires more coordination between team members because different individuals need to do different things at the same time.

In biological teams, "Teamwork" is used extensively for critical activities such as responding to a threat or exploiting an opportunity. We need to be able to use the different forms of teamwork effectively in our organizational teams, particularly for complex problem solving and situations, where real creativity is required.

Chapter Summary

There are 4 different types of teamwork exhibited by bioteams.

1. Solowork
2. Crowdwork
3. Groupwork
4. Teamwork

Each type of teamwork is appropriate at different times. A bioteam uses them all – each at the right time.

18. The three types of Recognition in bioteams

Three types of recognition in nature

There are three types of recognition in nature: Species Recognition, Kin Recognition and Individual Recognition.[42]

Bioteams can use Species Recognition to avoid freeloaders, Kin Recognition to build strong work-groups and Individual Recognition to ensure mutual team member cooperation.

Species Recognition: Species Recognition allows a bee or a monkey to recognize another bee or monkey. All species have this innate ability, however, they make mistakes. For example, ants are plagued by parasitic beetles that imitate ant signals and are admitted to and looked after by the colony. However they operate as "free-loaders" – they don't contribute.

Species recognition in a bioteam stops "freeloaders." In organizational teams this can be achieved through simple Ground Rules or Team Etiquette. Occasional freeloading should result in a gentle warning. Repeated freeloading should result in expulsion from the group.

For more on this see the Predator-Parasite Technique.

Kin Recognition: Kin Recognition allows a team member to know if another member is related to them.

This is important because, helping kin promotes an individual's gene pool, even if the individual does not benefit himself or herself. Kin recognition enables "kin selection," which explains acts of Altruism that would otherwise not happen according to "The Selfish Gene" theory. [42] While it is not universally agreed how kin recognition works in different species, it is believed that all species that live in social groups possess this ability.

As a general rule, collaborative outputs in organizational teams are produced by small groups and reviewed by bigger groups. The engine of these outputs is the small work-group or sub-group. Kin recognition can be implemented in an organizational team, by ensuring that the bigger team has the right set of tightly related sub-groups that operate well both in terms of individual relationships and complimentary skills.

Individual Recognition: Individual Recognition allows one individual member in a team to recognize another member.

Individual recognition is only present in nature's higher species such as primates or dolphins. Individual recognition is important in these teams because it enables mutual cooperation. I help you in the expectation that you will help me later. However, if I can't distinguish you, and you can't distinguish me from the other members of the team, then there is no way to return the compliment. Hence, mutual cooperative behavior does not evolve.

Research shows that if we don't know someone well, which is a risk in virtual relationships, we will find it easier to break commitments to them, and are unlikely to put ourselves out on their behalf. Individual Recognition can be implemented in an organizational team, by ensuring regular physical meetings as well as virtual ones. Also, we need to encourage good one on one virtual conversations, that build relationships as well as getting operational tasks done.

Chapter Summary

In our organizational teams we can learn from nature and ensure our team members use:

- Species Recognition to avoid freeloaders
- Kin Recognition to build strong work-groups
- Individual Recognition to ensure mutual cooperation

19. The three rings of commitment in a bioteam

One ring to rule them – one ring to bind them!

Managing any team, network or group becomes a whole lot simpler, if you understand the three rings of member commitment. I define the three rings as the Inner Ring, Middle Ring and Outer Ring. For something so fundamental, I was amazed to find that there seems to be very little written about it – the only reference I could find to anything vaguely similar is in, "Mastering Virtual Teams." [43] Biologically, this also fits well with the concept of message range in Pheromone Messaging, described in an earlier chapter.

The Three Rings

Essentially the group leader(s) and each group member should make a joint decision on which one of the three concentric rings of commitment they belong in (at that point in time):

The Inner Ring: This is where the leaders, and most committed group members, reside. This is also referred to as the Core Team, where the members are "accountable for direct task output."

The Middle Ring: This is where the normal active team members reside. This is also called the Extended Team, where there is not necessarily daily involvement from the members.

The Outer Ring: This is where the team members who make occasional input reside. This is also known as the Ancillary Team, whose role includes ad hoc expertise, reviewing and approving work.

Using the three rings

The three rings of a group make it very easy to discuss with team members, in simple terms, where everyone sits in terms of their commitment to the team. It also works very well with collaborative business networks, where team commitment is often the number one problem.

For each ring of the group, you just have to agree with its members on the following points:

- Types of communication
- Reply and response times
- Hours per week
- Involvement

You need all three rings!

Finally don't fall into the trap of thinking that Ring 3 members are less valuable than Ring 1 or Ring 2 members. You need all three rings operating well, in a successful team or network.

Ring 3 members can be absolutely crucial in areas such as authority, approvals, organizational grapevines and politics.

Chapter Summary

A much neglected aspect of group dynamics is that teams can usually be viewed in terms of three concentric rings of member commitment. This can be used to improve group organization and communications.

20. Using "Living Systems Theory"

Autopoiesis is the word!

With the explosion in software to support virtual teams, social networks and business cooperatives, it is amazing that so few people have realized that it is possible to treat these teams like living systems, and apply the well-respected philosophical principles of living systems (autopoiesis) to design for sustainability.

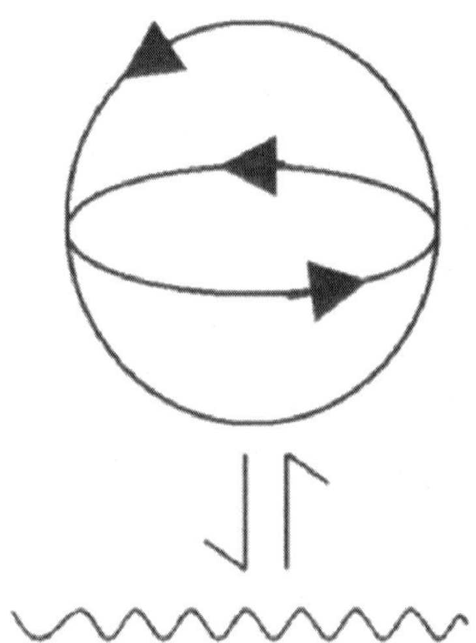

The theory of living systems was originally developed by Humberto Maturana and Francisco Varela, and is technically known as autopoiesis [30]. In essence, these two mould-breaking Chilean biologists argued that a living system should *not* be defined in terms of its attributes (e.g., growth or reproduction).

This ran totally counter to the common practice of the time.

Maturana and Varela wanted to define living systems in a more philosophically independent way, by suggesting that a living system is one, "whose only products are itself" – which is actually massively profound, if you really start to think about it.

They went on to suggest that there are four key aspects of any such living system represented graphically in the symbol above:

The Four components of a living system

1. *The Boundary:* Represented by the outer circle. The Boundary of a living system is open to energy but closed to foreign materials, i.e., it's a semi-porous boundary rather than a rigid boundary.
2. *The Processes:* Represented by the Arrow on the boundary to indicate that the boundary and the processes are one. The boundary is the 'being' and the processes are the "doing" of a living system. Living Systems Theory suggests, that a living system must have a complete set of processes within the system boundary to sustain itself, this is a crucial concept of sustainable systems design.
3. *The Nervous System:* Represented by the Inner Circle with the arrow. The Nervous system is the connection between external events and the internal processes of the living system.
4. *The Communication Channels:* Represented by the two arrows outside the main circle. This represents the 2-way communication between the living system and its external environment. Living systems are "plastic," which means that they co-evolve through communication with other living systems and their external environment.

My favorite example of co-evolution is feet and shoes: feet impact shoes (wear) and shoes impact feet (blisters).

The three nested levels of system within a team or group

I contend that we can apply living systems design to social systems, such as teams or groups or networks or communities, to transform them into bioteams.

Fritjof Capra, in his excellent and wide-ranging book, *The Hidden Connections,* [32] eloquently argues the case that social systems such as organizations and networks, are not just like living systems, they are living systems! Capra describes the five main metaphors that people have used to understand organizations:

1. Machines
2. Organisms
3. Brains

4. Cultures
5. Systems of government

He concludes that the fundamental debate is really whether we see our organizations as Machines (predictable) or Living Systems (unpredictable).

In an inspirational chapter, "Life and leadership in organizations," ([32] pp 85-112) Fritjof shows how a leader can address the key organizational and team challenges from a pure "living organization" perspective, including:

- Change Management
- Organizational Learning
- Novelty and Innovation
- Design and emergence
- Leadership
- Dignity

Now when we think of a social system such as a team there are really three nested systems:

1. The Individuals
2. The Groups the individuals belong to
3. The System the Groups belong to

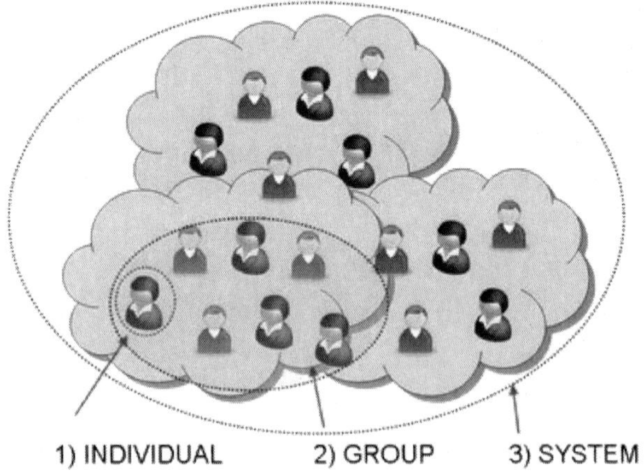

We have to apply Living Systems theory to each of these systems to determine if the overall system has the right components for sustainability.

Applying living systems concepts to social systems

For example, if we apply the Living System concepts at an individual level within a social system, the system components can be interpreted as follows:

1. *The Boundary:*
   ▪ Consider how well the individual's Identity and Reputation is defined and maintained.
   ▪ Consider how well the individual can manage both the Private space, and the different kinds of Open Space (to the rest of the group and beyond).
2. *The Processes:*
   ▪ Identify the processes that are available to each individual within the social system
   ▪ Establish if these processes form a complete set that meets the individuals needs (how do you know?).
3. *The Nervous System:*
   ▪ Identify the Events the individual wants to be notified about, plus any automated processes this could trigger.
   ▪ Is there a complete mapping between Events and Processes or are there missing events or processes?
4. *The Communication Channels*
   ▪ Identify the channels by which the individual can communicate with the other individuals, both within and outside the groups.
   ▪ Are they sufficient and appropriate?

In a similar manner, we can also interpret these concepts at the Group Level, in this case the four components each have different meanings. For example, The Boundary is about the Identity of the Group and the rules by which individuals may participate in the group (e.g., categories of membership with their rights and obligations).

When we apply the Processes Component at the Group System Level, it raises for me the question of roles in social networks and the interaction between them.

In Tom Quick's (University College London) excellent *Introduction to Autopoiesis* [44] he suggests that, "in crude terms a system is autopoietic if the bits and pieces of which it is composed, interact with each other in such a way as to continually produce, and maintain, that set of bits and pieces, and the relationships between them."

So, are your teams growing or dying?

I suggest that it is essential for teams to review their "systems" at all three levels, using the four living system components, to establish whether they meet the criteria for "living system" or not. They might be in for some surprises!

Chapter Summary

If we treat teams like living social systems, then we can apply the well-respected principles of living systems theory (autopoiesis), to transform them into bioteams.

21. "Requisite Variety" in bioteams

How do teams optimize for their environment?

An obvious characteristic of nature's best teams is that they seem to have just the right structure to handle their environments. Too much, and they would be slow and cumbersome; too little, and they would lack the sophisticated responses to protect their position in the food chain. This raises a number of big questions for human teams:

- How agile is your team to react to unexpected change?
- Is your team "over-structured" compared with its fast-moving external environment?
- How do you know if your team has the right amount of internal structure and relationships, to handle whatever its external environment is likely to throw at it?

The answer is the "Law of Requisite Variety." [45] In 1963, Ross Ashby formulated the law of Requisite Variety: when the variety or complexity of the environment exceeds the capacity of a system (natural or artificial), the environment will dominate and ultimately destroy that system.

The law tells us that a "system" only has "requisite variety," if its repertoire of responses is at least as big as the number of different stimuli it may encounter in its environment.

A system without requisite variety will fail whenever it encounters the unexpected, and as such is not a "viable system." We see examples of this all the time in business, where an enterprise with a limited set of responses is unable to react to unforeseen stimuli, due to a change in market conditions:

- *Inadequate variety:* If your environment is more sophisticated in terms of complexity than your team's available responses, then the moves will be simplistic and ineffective. This is inadequate variety, and is like trying to drive your car by moving the passenger's weights from side to side, because you don't have a steering wheel.
- *Excessive variety*: If, your team has too much structure, then it won't be agile or fast enough to react to changes in its

environment. This is excessive variety, and is like driving your car with such a complex dashboard, that you need to dual control it with a co-pilot!

How does nature achieve Requisite Variety?

The levers for achieving requisite variety are the same, whether it be a swarm of bees, or an ant colony, or a big cat hunting pack:

- *Mass* – enough members to cover the territory
- *Engagement* – members interact deeply in their local external environments
- *Randomness* – produces variety you might find unexpected "food"
- *Supporting Team Roles* – the team needs enough "foragers"

Randomness is also an important enabler of variety. For example, researchers have painstakingly produced foraging maps that show the directions an ant colony will forage each day over a period of many weeks. From this work they have learned that an established colony seems to have up to about eight foraging directions. On any day, however, it uses only three to five of them. So ant foraging embodies a randomness principle to support requisite variety.

More anecdotally, I have heard stories of African tribes, who start each day's hunt by effectively spinning a "sacred stick" to make a random choice of hunting direction. If they did not do this, they would be at a constant risk of "over hunting" certain territories that had been successful in the past, and missing out on new but unexpected food sources.

How can a human team achieve Requisite Variety?

Requisite Variety cannot be achieved by command and control! All teams face two important structural challenges in achieving requisite variety:

- *Cohesion* – allowing the members of a team to produce meaning beyond their personal needs.
- *Adaptation* – allowing the team to remain viable over time, in co-evolution with the key players in its external environment.

If these structural challenges are inadequately addressed, for example, through inappropriate command and control structures, then the team experiences what is known as "Control Dilemmas."

Espejo [46] puts it like this: "Management, having lower implementation variety than the autonomous units they control, cannot possibly maintain awareness of all that is going on within them. Yet, management knows that they are accountable for any loss of control. The anxiety to know more, leads to increased demands for special reports etc; however, in reality, these demands only serve to reduce the variety of autonomous units, making them less flexible, as they struggle to fulfill increased management requirements at the expense of carrying out their own operations. Because of the law of requisite variety, management in the cohesion function cannot win with this type of control strategy."

Amplification and Attenuation: Human teams have two options open to them in designing for requisite variety, Amplification and Attenuation.

- *Amplification:* Amplification is where the team sets up cooperation with other agents in its external environment, to amplify its ability to respond to stimuli. For example, an on-site IT support person is a way for the central IT Support Team to amplify its responses to a given customer.
- *Attenuation:* The objective of attenuation is, through sampling, to reduce the number of signals the system has to listen to. Examples of this include exception reporting and "managing by walking around."

Chapter Summary

Human teams can use the powerful concept of "Requisite Variety" to ensure they have the optimum structure for their environments. Too much structure or too little structure for the team environment will result in sub-optimal performance.

22. Ecosystems and bioteams

Three Key Ecosystem Concepts

Amazingly, a number of certain key concepts in biological ecosystems transfer immediately into the world of organizational teams. There are very important lessons we can use here from the ecology of biological networks and food webs described by Gerald Marten, [34] particularly:

- The "Community Assembly" Process
- The Three Types of relationships in a Food web
- The Complex interdependencies between species

Community Assembly

This is the name given to the process of self-organization within a biological community, which only admits a new species (business team or enterprise) into its "ecological niche," if it fits together in a "functional food web" with all the other species (customers, complementers and competitors) already there.

Community Assembly has three conditions that need to be fulfilled for a new species to be successfully incorporated in the community:

1. The new species must be adapted to the physical conditions at the site – think market.
2. The site must have the right kind of food and enough of it, for the new species to be able to grow and reproduce – think customers and resource partners.
3. If the site already has other animals that can eat the new species, then deaths cannot exceed births – think competitors and alternatives.

Food Web Relationships

Essentially three types of relationship exist between species in a food web:

1. Predator: e.g., Cats consume Mice
2. Competitor: e.g. Foxes and Cats eat Mice, Mice and Sheep eat Grass (competition for food or other resources)
3. Symbiont: e.g., Birds co-exist with Ticks for mutual benefit

In business and organizational terms, a new entity must identify the other main species in its web, and be able to establish which type of relationship exists or will be created – predator, competitor or symbiont.

When we think of competition we often only think of ecological predators, who compete for customers, and neglect ecological competitors who compete for vital resources such as staff.

In ecology, the roles of the other species are generally fixed. However, in the business and organizational worlds the roles an entity can play are much more fluid. For example, a company being a predator in one market, and a symbiont in another.

More importantly, these roles can be shaped as part of the new entity set-up, as at this stage most roles in the business ecosystem are only at a potential state. Therefore, the opportunity exists to consider how to convert potential powerful competitors into symbionts or at very least to less direct competitors within the ecosystem.

Complex interdependencies and feedback loops

These exist between species and the outcomes may be counter-intuitive and often only emerge over long periods of time.

For example, the relationships between prey and predator are described in *Ecology of Fear – Ecology of fear: Los Angeles and the imagination of disaster* [47]: "As settlers spread into the West, they killed vast numbers of animals, from grizzlies to mice, in an effort to make the wild more suitable for habitation. Hunting on this scale had a variety of effects on the rest of the ecosystem, and one of the best examples is that of hunting in the national game preserve of Arizona's Kaibab Plateau.

"As the number of humans in the area increased, the need (and the ability) to kill the predatory animals increased. In just over ten years 674 cougars, 3,000 coyotes and 120 bobcats were killed. As the number of predators available to kill the deer population decreased, so the number of deer increased. With almost all predators being wiped out, the deer population shot from around 3,000 in 1906 to over 100,000 in 1924. This increase meant the rate at which the local fauna was consumed similarly shot up, past its ability to regenerate itself.

"With the deer eating vegetation faster than it could grow, soon there was almost no food left, with the result that most of the deer swiftly died, leaving an expanse of largely bare (but predator-free) land."

In business and organizational terms, this principle applies equally well – for example if you go into a price war with your major competitor you are just as likely to destroy the profitability of the market for yourself as for them.

Another example would be destroying your major competitor, and then being perceived as having created a monopolistic situation, where your potential customers have no choice, and thereby causing a market or regulatory backlash.

Part 4: Measuring Bioteam Success

23. A team performance improvement scorecard

Realization of Bioteam's Benefits

It is vitally important that any team improvement initiative produce measurable benefits as well as qualitative ones. To achieve this, you need to know in advance where the likely benefit areas are, to enable you to focus on them, and track the degree to which they are realized or not.

To assist in the process of bioteams' benefits planning and realization, I have analyzed the potential impact of the 12 bioteaming rules on a team in terms of a) direct results [16] which could be produced and b) measurable benefits [21] these results would bring to a team.

Direct Results versus Benefits

Direct Results, indicated as Rx, are "leading indicators" that are necessary to produce the eventual benefit, and can be seen and measured before the benefit itself (which is known as a "lagging indicator" and marked as Bx).

Leading indicators let you know whether things are going in the right direction or not. A good test of a leading indicator is how early you can see it. For more on the difference between leading and lagging indicators see *The Balanced Scorecard* by Robert Kaplan and David Norton. [48]

The Overall Bioteam's Measurement Process in Context

The overall bioteam's benefits planning and realization process follows the following steps:

- Identify top result and benefit areas.
- Establish current performance for each area.
- Estimate new performance possible in each areas using

bioteaming

- Financially, value the performance enhancement for each area
- Select the key indicators to track.
- Track the early results and estimated benefits during the project, and make adjustments in approach as required.
- Measure the benefits post-project.
- Compare the actual benefits with the estimated benefits and explain any differences.

Once you have identified the potential direct results and benefits, next you need to estimate the financial impact of each of these benefits on the specific team. To do this, the team needs to identify its current performance in each of these areas, estimate its new performance using bioteams, and place a financial value on the difference. Based on this analysis, a team should identify a small number of measures that it will use to assess the impact of bioteaming. Key factors in choosing a measure include the quality of its leading indicator, and the degree of scope for significant improvement in the current team performance level.

The Bioteam's model scorecard – Leadership Zone

Rule 1: Stop Controlling

Communicate information not orders.

This should visibly result in:

R1 – Reduced Command and Control Overheads.

R2 – Reduced Waiting Time for team members waiting for orders.

The measurable benefits of this are:

B1 – Better Utilization of leadership time.

B2 – Improved Team Productivity.

Rule 2: Team Intelligence/Broadcast

Mobilize everyone to look for and manage team threats and opportunities.

This should visibly result in:

R3 – Less Trivial Non-Value-Adding, 2-way communications.

R4 – Quicker Identification of Threats and Opportunities.

The measurable benefits of this are:

B3 – More Project Opportunities taken.
B4 – Less Project Showstoppers impacting team outcomes.

Rule 3: Permission Granted

Achieve accountability through transparency, not permission.

This should visibly result in:
R5 – Improved Team Member Ownership.
R6 – Improved Team Member Capability, Development and Growth.

The measurable benefit of this is:
B5 – Better utilization of leadership time (cf B1).

The Bioteam's model scorecard – Connectivity Zone

Rule 4: Always On

Provide 24*7 instant "in-situ" message hotlines for all team members

This should visibly result in:
R7 – Team members able to respond quicker.

The measurable benefit of this is:
B6 – Improved Team Productivity and Responsiveness.

Rule 5: Symbiosis

Treat external partners as fully trusted team members

This should visibly result in:

R8 – More creative co-invention with partners rather than traditional develop-review cycle.

The measurable benefits of this are:

B7 – Higher degree of radical and breakthrough innovations and problem solving in team.

B8 – Finding out quicker that proposed products/processes do not work.

Rule 6. Cluster

Nurture the team's internal and external networks and connections

This should visibly result in:

R9 – Better linkages and relationships with project customers, suppliers and external parties, that the team depends on, in some way.

The benefits of this are:

B9 – Reduced time between an external event happening and the team being able to take the appropriate action or change in direction.

B10 – Less effort and more chance of being successful in getting external parties, to quickly take unplanned action on behalf of team.

The Bioteam's model scorecard – Execution Zone

Rule 7: Swarm:

Develop consistent autonomous team member behaviors.

This should visibly result in:

R10 – Problems/Threats spotted earlier.

R11 – Better/Quicker team mobilization to address spotted Problems/Threats .

The measurable benefit of this is:

B11 – Less nasty surprises discovered too late to fix without impact.

Rule 8: Tit-for-Tat

Teach team members effective biological personal cooperation strategies.

This should visibly result in:

R12 – Less festering unresolved interpersonal team issues.

The measurable benefits of this are:

B12 – Better team member motivation and less team politics.

B13 – Better team member utilization – less time spent in non-value-adding activities.

Rule 9: Genetic Algorithms

Learn through experimentation, mutation and team review.

This should visibly result in:

R13 – Less effort and time expended going down blind alleys

The measurable benefits of this are:

B14 – Finding out quicker that proposed products/processes do not work (cf B8).

B15 – Specific deliverables should be right, with less overall effort, less time and less testing effort.

The Bioteam's model scorecard – Organization Zone

Rule 10: Self-Organizing Networks

Define the team in terms of "network transformations" – not outputs.

This should visibly result in:

R13 – Better relationships with external parties (suppliers and customers) (cf R9).

The measurable benefits of this are:

B15 – Less impact on project due to planned and unexpected supplier dependencies, as they will be more flexible.

B16 – Less impact on project due to customer requirements and scope inflexibilities, as they will be more flexible.

Rule 11: Porous Membranes

Develop team boundaries that are open to energy but closed to waste.

This should visibly result in:

R14 – Less team members who will behave in an uncommitted, selfish, or free-loading way.

The measurable benefits of this are:

B17 – Less effort required by leaders to police commitments.

B18 – Better commitment management.

B19 – Less resentment in team regarding freeloaders.

Rule 12. Emerge

Scale naturally through nature's universal growth and decay cycles.

This should visibly result in:

R15 – Less team members sitting around without useful work.

R16 – Less resourcing mistakes.

The measurable benefits of this are:

B20 – More efficient use of resources (cf B13).

B21 – Less management required of non-productive resources.

Summary Scorecard

In the table below, I have summarized the benefits of each of the first six bioteam rules, and how these benefits can be measured and valued:

Leadership Zone

Rule	Results	Benefits	Measured	Financial Valued?
Rule 1 Provide Information not Orders	Reduced Command and Control Overheads Reduced waiting time/project latency/ waiting for approval	Improved Team Productivity	Deadline Performance % Original Scope Delivery % Original Benefits Realization	Yes – take from the original project business case. Each feature carries a monthly benefit value to each commercial organization in the project. Delays and descoping of project features have a directly measurable cost.
Rule 2 Permission Granted: Accountability through Transparency Systems	Improved Team Member Ownership Improved Team Member Capability Development	More time available to team leaders and members to spend on strategic and innovative work	Work Value Profile (= Strategic/ Time as % of Total Time which includes 1. Rework, 2 Operations and 3 Strategic)	Yes, not directly but via impact on Improved Team Productivity. (Typically staff have a 40/40/20 profile but could become 15/25/60 - 3 times better)
Rule 3 Everybody gathers/ broadcasts intelligence and less 2-way messaging	Less trivial/non-value-adding communications Quicker Identification and reaction to Threats and Opportunities	More Project Showstoppers and Opportunities spotted earlier in time to do something about them	Project Stage profile of showstopper identification % showstoppers impact avoided Number of opportunities realized within the project	Yes, not directly but via impact on Improved Team Productivity plus Cost Avoidance on overtime/use of contract staff to try and overcome showstoppers spotted late.

Connectivity Zone

Rule	Results	Benefits	Measured	Financial Valued?
Rule 4 Always On: Instant "in situ" com-munca-tions	Agility - ability to respond quicker to the unexpected	Increased External Project Team Member and Organization Satisfaction with Project	Specific Personal Feedback Willingness to engage in next project Improved payback for their organizational	Yes. For Customer Partners can be measured in willingness to commit to future revenue-earning projects. For Supplier partners willingness to 'play again' reduces the next project's risk and thus improves Team Productivity
Rule 5 Out-Team: Symbioses with External Partners	More creative co-invention with partners rather than sequential work	Less Rework	Reduced number of cycles before a deliverable is acceptable	Yes, not directly but via impact on Improved Team Productivity plus Cost Avoidance on overtime/use of contract staff to do the rework
		Higher degree of radical / novel / breakthrough innovations and problem solving	Increased % of successful project solutions which are non-incremental/ new design	Yes, not directly but via impact on Improved Team Productivity plus Cost Reduction/Revenue of project innovations and inventions
Rule 6 Nurture the Network: Develop Project Network Connectivity	Better Linkages with Project Customers and external parties the Project depends on	Reduced time between an environmental /requirements change or issue occurring and the project changing its direction to accommodate it	Reduction in time/effort wasted between issue occurring and project knowing about it	Yes, not directly but via impact on Improved Team Productivity plus Cost Avoidance on overtime/use of contract staff which was avoidable.
		Reduced time and hassle in getting external parties (both inside and outside the organization) to do unplanned things for the project	Average resolution time involving external parties Reduction in slips due to unexpected ext. dependencies	Yes, not directly but via impact on Improved Team Productivity plus Cost Avoidance on overtime/use of contract staff. on work-arounds/ negotiations

Part 5: Seven Key Bioteaming Techniques

24. Introduction to the Bioteam Techniques

Why, what, who, how and when?

Having a good theory is necessary for success but it is not sufficient.. In other words you also need a set of practical proven techniques for turning the current reality into the desired reality.

Before they get into anything "business critical," a bioteam must get five things straight:

1. WHY should we work together?
2. WHAT should we do together?
3. WHO should do what?
4. HOW should we work together?
5. WHEN do we need to act in certain ways?

Here are my seven key bioteaming techniques for addressing these questions. You will notice that each technique addresses not one, but two or three of the five questions – they are designed like this to ensure they interlock and cross-check each other.

Technique Matrix

TECNIQUES/FOCUS	Why	What	Who	How	When
T1 - Symbiosis (Team Synergy Discovery)	X	X			
T2 - Predator-Parasite (Ground Rules)			X	X	
T3 – Metabolism (Team Karma)		X	X		
T4 - Swarming (Autonomy & Responsibility)				X	X
T5 - Tit for Tat (Personal Collaboration Strategies)				X	X
T6 - Team Ties (Social Network Analysis)			X		X
T7 - Cell Division (Effective sub work groups)	X	X			

There is no standard bioteams roadmap

I do not believe in a team improvement roadmap or cookbook, with a standard set of interventions to be made to a team, in a predefined sequence to make it a bioteam. In my experience, this simply does not work.

The best way to use any of these techniques is "just-in-time," in the context of a current problem or opportunity.

The only other guidelines I can offer are these:

- Techniques T1-T3 are *foundational* – they should generally be used in the team mobilization stages.
- Techniques T4-T7 are *operational* – they should generally be used in the team execution stages.

Technique T1: Symbiosis

Symbiosis

An ongoing close cooperation between two or more independent living organisms for mutual gain.

Purpose

To discover the critical synergies and gaps in a team that are normally very well hidden.

Objectives

To find if real collaboration opportunities exist within a potential team:

- Identify any critical gaps that could derail the team.
- Create new and effective win-win partnerships within a team.

Background

The conventional approach to working with a new team or group is to first build some trust, exchange relevant information and then start exploring collaboration possibilities. The problem is that this approach does not really work!

The first problem is that it usually takes far too long, never gains enough momentum or continuity, and eventually the participants lose interest and move on to "something productive."

The second major problem is: Let's imagine you have invested in building "enough trust" with the group, and then you find that after all this effort and time, you don't actually have the right people in the team. By then it is too late!

How to use it

The main objective of "Instant Network" is to find out if there are enough potential synergies within the group to make it work.

The other objective, which is just as important, is to do this very quickly in a way that is highly interactive, engaging, and develops new relationships.

In addition, I always try and send each participant away with at least one new useful relationship, even if they never come to another bioteam meeting.

Here is an example of how I have used the Symbiosis technique, with a group of independent businesses who wanted to explore the benefits of collaboration:

In this case I used the following six key roles that can easily be adapted for a single enterprise team:

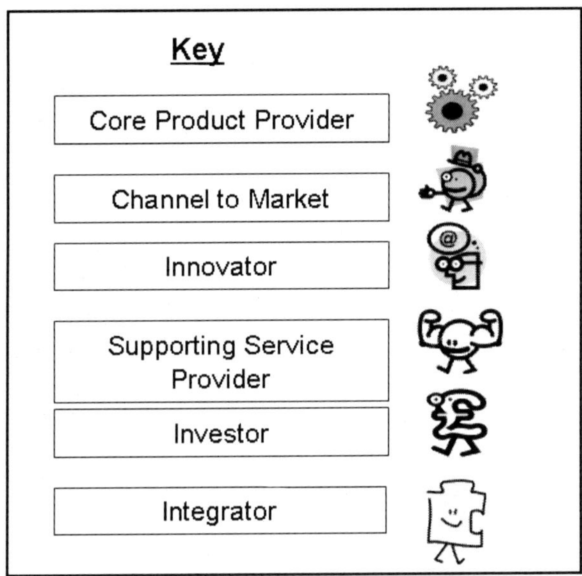

Step1: Everyone identifies their core business offer, and put it on a YELLOW card with their name, and stick it up on a large white-board. I call these YELLOW cards, Core Product Providers.

Step2: Everyone reads all the cards, and must fill out at least one BLUE card and stick it beside any Core Product card (YELLOW), that they believe they might be able to produce for a new customer. I call these BLUE cards, Channels.

Step3: Everyone also fills out at least one PURPLE card for any YELLOW card, that they believe they have some knowledge of, or a product that could make a core product more valuable. They stick up these too beside the YELLOW Core Product cards. I call these PURPLE cards, Innovators.

Step4: We examine the whiteboard and see how many natural sub-clusters are made up of Core Product Providers, one or more Channels and one or more Innovators can be found.

Step5: I then ask the participants to look for opportunities to merge these sub-clusters with the objective of having not more than 3 merged clusters. Also each merged cluster should have least

4 players, one of whom should be a channel or it is not viable.

Step6: I then ask the participants to go back to work on these merged clusters, to explore the possibilities and requirements for three further roles, and they stick more cards into the clusters on the whiteboard for:

- RED – Supporting Service Provider - provides a critical supporting service for the collaborative product.
- ORANGE – Integrator - plays a key design or integration role in the new collaborative product.
- GREY – Investor - can provide finance or resources needed to make the collective supply chain viable, and attractive to the market.

Step7: We then do a quick "tidy up," to name and assess scope for each of the merged clusters, as "collaborative product offers." Then we close-out by seeking feedback from each of the participants to see if they are intrigued enough to want to collaborate further to develop each of the merged clusters.

Technique T2: Predator-Parasite (PP)

Predator-Parasite

- *Predator:* A creature whose existence depends on consuming another living organism.
- *Parasite:* A creature whose existence depends on consuming resources provided by another living organism.

Purpose

Agreeing to real and effective team ground rules, to guard against predators who will destroy the team, and parasites (a.k.a., free-loaders) who will exhaust the team and contribute nothing.

Background

It is important for a Team to establish ground rules on how it intends to operate. In my approach to teams I split this into two:

- Ground Rules – the negative team member behaviors we wish to discourage.

- Team Culture and Behaviors – the positive team member and group behaviors we wish to encourage and adopt. Team Culture and Behaviors are covered in Technique

Objectives

Ground Rules are the agreed position of the whole team regarding what behaviors are mandatory, and what action should be taken, if this is not the case (warnings and sanctions). Ground Rules must be short, sharp, unambiguous and unanimously agreed, otherwise they cannot be enforced by the team.

A Ground Rules document should never exceed two pages of letter-size paper.

WARNING: Most teams set the standards too high for their ground rules. These kinds of unrealistic ground rules quickly become discredited, as most people don't comply with them, and then it can be very hard to put in any ground rules whatsoever. A weak set of ground rules implemented, is always better than a great set of ground rules not implemented.

Ground Rules are meaningless if not implemented. This means that, warnings and sanctions have to happen early on, or else the ground rules are not worth the paper they are written on. To enable this to happen you need to make it an embarrassment, or black mark, to be warned or face sanctions. This is where you can lead by example, by letting yourself receive an early sanction for the sake of the team!

How to use it

Step 1: Agree to the Ground Rules Checklist (here is my tried and tested checklist):

1. *Trust Damagers:* What will damage trust?
2. *Trust Destroyers:* What will destroy trust?
3. *Conflicts of Interest:* What are the most likely scenarios to arise and how should they be handled?
4. *Team Boundaries/Member Types:* What are the boundaries of the team and types of member participation (e.g., Core, Reviewer, Expert, Other)?
5. *Information Sharing:* Where to be transparent and where to be private?

6. *Issue/Conflict Resolution*: How will we resolve issues/conflicts, and what will be the main stages in this practice?
7. *Decision Making Practices:* How will we make decisions in the main categories: Strategic: Wide Operational (affects most project members), Narrow: Operational (affects only a few project members)?
8. *Meetings:* What will be the team meetings? Purpose, frequency, attendees and channels (face to face, phone, online)?
9. *Induction/Mentoring/Buddying:* How will we handle new team members joining?
10. *Communications Tools:* Which tools will we use for which type of communications (urgent, important), and what will be the agreed "Reply by" Times?
11. *Sanctions:* What sanctions will we employ and how will we agree on them? Red Card/Yellow Card or Penalty Points?

Step 2. Conduct Ground Rules Team Session#1: Allow 90 minutes to use the check-list, as a means of asking each member of the team their opinion.

Never do it as a group discussion, you need the individual inputs from every team member.

An electronic meeting tool that allows everyone to type their answers and see other members' answers is the best environment for doing this. After each answer you should summarize the key themes, and ask supplementary questions if you need more details.

Step 3. Document the Session: There are two outputs, the unedited log of what everyone said, plus a document that summarizes the session question by question, and identifies clearly:

- Where the group was in agreement
- Where the group was not in agreement (or answered in insufficient depth to be able to know)

This second document requires excellent editing skills to ensure it exposes the critical points of disagreement, and where there is insufficient clarity/definition. It is a summary, and should not exceed three pages.

Step 4. Include review comments: Circulate both documents to the participants (typically with the full transcript as an appendix to the summary) and request comments.

Where a comment is a simple, non-contentious clarification, or a correction, update the document accordingly.

Where a comment is contentious, or represents a further elaboration on what was said at the meeting, include it in the document in a way that makes this clear. Re-circulate the updated document.

Step 5. Conduct Ground Rules Team Session#2: Allow 90 minutes, then work through the document again, question by question.

Request quick confirmation from team on all agreed questions, don't open these up to further discussion.

Request more discussion on other points, to try and identify an agreed position.

If discussion is not productive after a maximum of 5-10 minutes, identify two extreme positions that cover both ends of the argument, and if necessary, do an informal vote

Don't try and 'wordsmith' the document as a group, capture the key points and 'wordsmith' it later.

It is OK to leave a couple of items as unresolved, *provided they are not central,* it's better to do this, than to get the whole group stuck and unable to proceed.

Step 6. Document the Session and Reissue Revised Document: Where necessary in this version, identify two options on points that are not yet agreed to, and request that people indicate their preference. If the group is split, then leave both options in the document for review later. It generally becomes obvious which will work best. Publish the final document as Version 1.0 with the date, a living document.

Step 7. Schedule Regular Ground Rules Discussion Items: Ensure a Ground Rules item is included in one full team meeting per month. The discussion should be — Are we having any compliance issues? If not, then move quickly on to the next agenda item.
If yes:
1) Is it a misunderstanding?
<u>Or</u>

2) Are the Ground Rules unrealistic in this area and require change?
Or
3) Do we need to implement the agreed warnings and sanctions?

Technique T3: Team Metabolism

Metabolism

The process through which a living organism converts food into energy and waste.

Purpose

Determining the Team 'Karma,' what member's want and what they will contribute to get it!

Objectives

To balance personal team member expectations with inputs.

Background

If an organism takes in insufficient food, it will eventually wither and die. If a team has insufficient resources, it will eventually share the same fate. All the evidence shows that team members typically want to get more out of a team than they are prepared to put in.

The purpose of Team Metabolism is to confront the team with this reality, so that they can take action before it is too late.

How to use it

Step 1: Articulate your view of the VISION for the team (ending with some real concrete specifics).

Step 2: Communicate the vision to the team at a Team Session (*Workshop 1*). Don't go into a group discussion on it, that will come later. Then outline the process you will be following with them (not in any detail), to see where (if anywhere), they fit.

Step 3: Request they individually email you their comments on your vision (what they like, don't like, think is missing – not questions!). Also, what specifically they wish to get out of working with you (part 1 of Karma).

Step 4: Consolidate this for yourself and see how it looks.

Step 5: Develop a list of the *top 20 tasks* that will have to be done, to deliver the VISION. Group the tasks into the relevant roles (part 2 prep of Karma). In the LANCELOT case study, there's an example from a bioteam of international language trainers, who wished to form a collaborative network.

Step 6: Create the *karma spreadsheet* you can use, to gather and consolidate the info.

Step 7: Have another team meeting (*workshop 2*) to present back their comments on your vision (and how you may have adjusted it), their consolidated wants (not identifying individuals), and explain the spreadsheet.

Step 8: Now request each team member individually, to indicate what they will take responsibility for on this list, by filling out the spreadsheet (Karma part 2 execution). There are 3 options for each task:

- I am prepared to lead this
- I am prepared to be an active team member in this, but not to lead
- I will help out if I have the time (in reality, zero commitment)

Step 9: Consolidate their inputs (Karma part 2), and see for yourself what the gaps are. Here's an example from a bioteam of independent small businesses, who formed a collaborative business network, for joint bidding and product development.

PART2 - MEMBER INPUTS	Lead	Participate	Contribute
B1 Bring Opportunities to Network – from existing contacts	0	5	5
B2 Bring Opportunities to Network – not existing contacts (e.g. cold call, tender scanning.)	1	2	7
B3 Ensuring all potential tender opportunities are properly investigated to closure or bid	1	4	5

B4 Secure and conduct prospective customer meetings (initial and follow-up)	2	3	5
B5 Prepare and conduct network sales presentations	0	2	6
B6 Prepare Formal written Bids, Responses and Proposals	0	5	3
B7 Negotiate/Organize Commercial Term for specific Network Bids	0	2	4
B8 Conduct Market Research on markets, customers, geographies & products	0	3	5

Step 10: Have a team session (*Workshop 3*) where you present it to them, along with the consequences. At the end of it, request that they make their new "offers" to you, and that you will select your team on that basis.

Step 11: Receive their *new offers* and see if they cover enough for you to fly!

Step 12: Assuming they do, have 1:1 conversations with your team members to finalize and commit their new offers.

Technique T4: Swarming

Swarming

Exceptionally agile group coordination while on the move (also known as flocking).

Purpose

To create a healthy balance between Autonomy and Responsibility in team members, c*reate controlled self-management in your team.*

Objectives

Identify the key stimuli the team must respond to.

Identify the key responses that must be produced.

Background

Almost all team leaders want their teams to take more ownership and initiative. However, team leaders may shy away from "self-managed" teams, because of a perception that this would be an abdication of their leadership, or the fear of it leading to anarchy and chaos.

This technique identifies 7-generic behaviors of "responsible autonomous team members" that can be discussed and refined to suit the specific team, members, environment and objectives.

Craig Reynolds, a computer graphics researcher, studied how bird flocks fly in formation, to see whether there were simple rules that could be simulated by computer software.

As a group activity, "flocking" is extremely complex. However, it turns out that it can be explained by just three simple, underlying member behaviors.

How to use it

Today's common wisdom, on creating high performance teams, is that you need to create a team environment where the individual members can fully exercise their creativity and innovation. This is very true, but I believe that nature's teams show us that it is only half of the story of high performing teams.

When we use the normal approach to high performing teams, we are actually jumping to the higher team capability level of "complex individual behavior," but skipping out the lower team capability level of "simple but highly consistent individual behavior."

In so doing, we sacrifice a number of important benefits by not putting this foundation platform in place first, because nature's examples prove that coordinated individual simple behavior can produce more intelligent collective responses, than un-coordinated individual complex behavior.

Now obviously, human teams are not going to gain much benefit from the kind of rules that ants or geese use.

Human team members have the gift of human intelligence, so we need to construct rules that are more abstract, and allow space for team members to apply their own judgments.

O-R-G-A-N-I-C team member behaviors

I would suggest the following seven behavior rules as a discussion starter, for beginning to develop consistent, autonomous member behavior in your teams:

1. *Outgoing* – get to know all your team colleagues
2. *Recruit* – look out for new external partners to strengthen the team's network
3. *Go!* – network widely outside the team
4. *Ask* – constantly ask for and offer help to other team members
5. *Note* – keep aware/abreast of issues of "team intelligence"
6. *Investigate* -when you see something interesting, investigate it for the team
7. *Collaborate* – join at least one team workgroup as an active member; don't just be a "reviewer"

Develop the Team Stimulus-Response Code

A good way to develop the team stimulus-response code is, to first list and prioritize the key stimuli that the team must respond to, each of these are either THREATS or OPPORTUNITIES. They can also be classified as Urgent/Not Urgent. Next identify the ideal response a team should make. There are three types of team responses:

1. Any member can respond
2. All members must respond
3. Specific members only must respond

Finally you can use the ORGANIC checklist to see if you have missed anything.

Technique T5: Tit for Tat (TFT)

Tit for Tat

Nature's most effective strategy for successful, long-term collaboration between two independent organisms.

Purpose

Teach team members viable, long-term, and personal collaboration strategies, that enable them (unlike Win-Win) to fully recover from non-cooperative interventions by their fellow team members.

Objectives

Most team members don't have a practical technique for what they do, when another team member lets them down. "Win – Win" is an outcome, not an effective collaboration strategy.

Without a personal collaboration strategy, many team members inevitably feel taken advantage of by others, and just "silently disengage" from the team, in terms of their commitment and participation.

This technique uses nature's most effective collaboration strategy, "Tit for Tat."

Background

Research has discovered that many species in nature use a surprising strategy for cooperation, known as TIT FOR TAT (TFT).

The rules of TFT are very simple – cooperate, unless and until the other party does not the retaliate, then cooperate again.

How to use it

Recent research has shown that TIT FOR TAT is also the best, long-term strategy for human cooperation.

Human teams and their members often say that they are committed to *playing* "Win-Win," which is great! But what does this actually mean?

I propose that the best strategy for achieving Win-Win is not Win-Win but in fact TIT FOR TAT!

Team members who say they are playing 'win-win' are generally referring to one of two very different, personal collaboration strategies:

Mr. Nice Guy: "I will assume you are cooperating with me, until it is proven you are not, then I won't work with you again."

In this situation you can be easily taken advantage of, at which point you are too resentful to try and put it right. Relationships that start in this kind of naivety generally end in tears!

Mr. Stand-off: "I will assume you are not cooperating, until it is proven you are. And if it is not conclusively proven after a certain time, I will assume (privately) you are not a good partner."

Relationships that start in this kind of distrust, usually become self-fulfilling prophecies, start cautiously and you won't be disappointed!

Win-Win is a state, not a strategy

So Win-Win is actually a highly desirable outcome/state, but is itself not the best strategy for getting there. Because, Win-Win (in both forms above) has no means of checking a non-cooperating partner, and then recovering team members need practical, personal collaboration strategies such as TFT, based on four simple principles:

1. Never be the first to defect
2. Retaliate only after your partner has defected
3. Be prepared to forgive after carrying out just one act of retaliation
4. Make it clear to all your team members that these are the rules you go by, secret TFT does not work!

Absence of such strategies creates distrust that results in a huge amount of waste such as:

- People checking up on each other
- Team members falling out
- People playing politics
- Members raising personality issues with the leader rather than the offending person
- Email wars
- Team cliques

Consistent use of TFT in a team by its members will avoid all this.

Technique T6: Team Ties

Team Ties

Team ties play a crucial role in our ability to communicate with the outside world. For an excellent introduction to "Social Network Analysis," see Rob Cross and Andrew Parkers' excellent book, *The Hidden Power of Social Networks.* [49]

Purpose

To identify the key external relationships needed for the team's success, and to establish who are the best team members, and to look for them.

Objectives:

- Who do the team need good external connections with?
- Who on the team holds any relevant relationships?
- Where is the team collectively missing crucial relationships?
- What actions are required to a) nurture existing relationships and b) develop new relationships?

Background

Conventionally, two assumptions are made in teams:

- It is the "leader's" job to manage all external relationships.
- All team members are relationally equal.

Both these assumptions are *wrong*. First, *It is the leader's job to manage all external relationships.* Relationships are living things and are never binary, on or off. They are qualitative and reflect years of interaction and trust. Therefore, it is nearly always better to develop an existing relationship held by a more junior team member, than to expect the leader to rapidly build all key relationships themselves, from scratch.

Second, *All team members are relationally equal.* Research shows that a few team members will have much better external connections, *known as weak ties*, than the average team member. We need to identify these members of the team, and work with them to use these relationships to the team's advantage.

Effective teams have good internal and external networks

Social Network Analysis research identifies two basic types of relationship – Weak and Strong Ties. Organizational teams tend to be biased to one form of tie or the other. They seldom manage both well, naturally.

Strong ties are very good for getting work done, usually in small tightly bound groups. But such teams are not generally known for their skills at listening to, and responding to, the signals from and changes in their external or customer environments.

Weak ties (hubs or connectors) are very good for listening, but not great for getting things actually done.

The importance of strong ties in teams

It can often be a mistake to try and create work in groups that are too large, in the hope that this will ensure everybody is heard and brought-in. Large groups can be effective, but only if they are very carefully managed to ensure that the collaboration is not dominated by only a few.

Some electronic meeting tools can be very effective here, if used properly. However, this is the exception rather than the rule. The trick is to create the core collaborative product, using the smallest effective group, but to leave enough headroom and flexibility in it, for the wider group to fully contribute and collaborate, in its review and extension. This is addressed further in the bio-technique – Cell Division.

The importance of weak ties in teams

Looser relationships exist between the different smaller groups within a team that connect them to each other, and connect the team to its outside partners. Typically these connections are between the hub members of each small group. A team without such a structure of weak ties is vulnerable to duplication of effort and poor coordination. Such a team may be the "last to know" of important changes in its environment.

An example of this is, the great "heads-down" technical team that produces an excellent report that is not actually used because it is no longer needed (but nobody told them).Or, it was delivered to such a high specification, that it arrived just too late to be useful.

How to use it

Phase 1: The team needs to map out their collective networks and identify gaps. This involves asking the following questions:

1. Who are the communities the team will impact?
2. What is the nature of the impact ?
    a) community is a customer for team (positive or negative?)
    b) community is a resource for the team NB – communities can be in both categories
3. What kinds of players does the team need in each community?
    a) Intelligence Providers
    b) Resource Providers
    c) Authority Providers
4. What names can the team propose for these players?

5. What kind of relationships are in place between team members and these players?
   a) None
   b) weak (weak tie)
   c) strong (strong tie)
   d) positive, negative or neutral
6. How do these relationships need to be managed by the team and by which member?

Phase 2: The team needs to create and nurture this network.

The ideal network for the team will support two objectives, getting the job done right (strong ties), and getting the right job done (weak ties).

The team must address both its *external* and *internal network*. There are two priorities internally – ensuring need effective sub-groups (strong ties), and ensuring the team has the right internal hubs (weak ties).

When the social network analysis is done, it often reveals that only one person in a team holds many vital relationships. What happens if they get sick or overloaded? Where is the fault tolerance? Also sometimes, these people are not the best ones to be holding these relationships! Hubs are also vital for ensuring the team gets 'team intelligence' early enough to use it. *Customer Hubs are very important,* but many teams neglect other equally critical hubs such as:

1. Technical Hubs (who can get the IT department to do you favors)
2. Social Hubs (who know the team's temperament)
3. Organizational Hubs (who are very well connected to the company grapevine at a high level)

Technique T7: Cell Division

Cell Division

It is the process by which a cell divides, and upon completion of the process, each daughter cell contains the same genetic material as the original cell.

Purpose

To find the smallest viable sub-group, for making something happen in a larger team or group.

Objectives

To identify the key subgroups a bigger team needs (3 max). To resource these in the optimum way in terms of ownership, autonomy and team size.

Background

Research shows that Working Groups should be between 5 and 9 people.

Below this, they lack resources, are unstable or spilt into factions.

Above this, team members don't get enough individual attention, due to lack of time for grooming, to maintain relationships. Teams start to work again when they reach around 25, as it becomes possible to spilt them up into distinct sub-teams of 5 to 9.

This also broadly agrees with a finding in one of my favorite books, *The Mythical Man Month* [19] by Fred Brooks, who was a pioneer in discovering the unexpected burden it places on team communications, when new members are added to teams.

This work resulted in the famous maxim, often referred to as Brooks Law, that "adding resource to a late software project only makes it later."

How to use it

Identify the key work areas needed for a group to succeed. For much more on this, see the Symbiosis technique described earlier.

- Seek volunteers to a) lead or b) be a pro-active team member in each group
- Review each subgroup for a) missing leaders b) missing team members and c) critical mass
- Identify if a subgroup has too many members, since this will destroy its dynamic
- Help the group collectively build a Terms of Reference (See CTSL Case Study for a good example)
- Support and Encourage each work group to deliver against its own plan and objectives

Part 6: Bioteaming Case Studies

25. Overview of Case Studies

The table below shows how the case studies illustrate the main bioteaming rules:

ETC: Virtual Enterprise Network
DaisyHill: Hospital Intermediate Care Team
CTSL: Telecoms Industry Working Party
DK: Conference Organization
LAN: Virtual Language School
K45: Music Fan Engagement

Main Rules	**ETC**	**Daisy Hill**	**CTSL**	**DK**	**LAN**	**K45**
1 Stop Controlling			X		X	
2 Team Intelligence		X				
3 Permission Granted						
4 Always On	X	X		X		X
5 Symbiosis				X	X	X
6 Cluster				X		X
7 Swarm	X					
8 Tit for Tat					X	
9 Genetic Algorithms						X
10 Self-Organizing Networks			X			
11 Porous Membranes	X					
12 Emerge						X

ETC: Virtual Enterprise Network

1. The Bioteam

Environmental Technologies Cluster (ETC)

The team comprises fifteen core member companies operating in the Environmental Technologies Sector, and located on the border between Northern and Southern Ireland.

ETC is a cross border consortium of innovative specialist companies in the following areas:

- Waste Water Services
- Bioremediation
- Testing & Analysis
- Waste Management
- Environmental Consultancy

2. Background and Context

As small businesses, the member companies found that they were often excluded from winning large contracts, because they were individually perceived as being too small. They decided to come together to form a Virtual Enterprise Network (VEN), with the strong support of *INVEST NI*, the regional enterprise development agency. This offered them the scale and resources of a major company, but still retaining the agility and cost base of small businesses. Member companies currently export to Asia, Europe, America and Australia, and their collective employment is in excess of 300 personnel, and combined annual turnover is in excess of £34 million. (For more on the VEN concept see, "A Taxonomy of Virtual Business Networks" on *www.bioteams.com* [50] and related papers on the site).

3. Objectives

The specific objective for companies was, to strengthen their ability to compete on a global commercial stage, by creating a critical mass to enable them to realize their collective strength and individual potential, particularly through collective tendering, joint marketing, joint purchasing and joint R&D.

It was intended that the companies (as well as operating their normal business activities) should come together to define and construct a joint collaborative offer to the market. For example, a "one-stop-shop," or an innovative new bundling of existing environmental products and services.

4. How bioteaming was used

There are three critical dimensions in a Virtual Enterprise Network:

- Network Development/Governance
- Member/Capability Development
- Business/Market Development

To succeed, a network needs to be able to develop all 3 dimensions in parallel. Often, one of these is emphasized at the expense of the other two, and the network gets fragmented. The diagram below shows the main tasks the team members identified, in the critical incubation phase for each of the three dimensions.

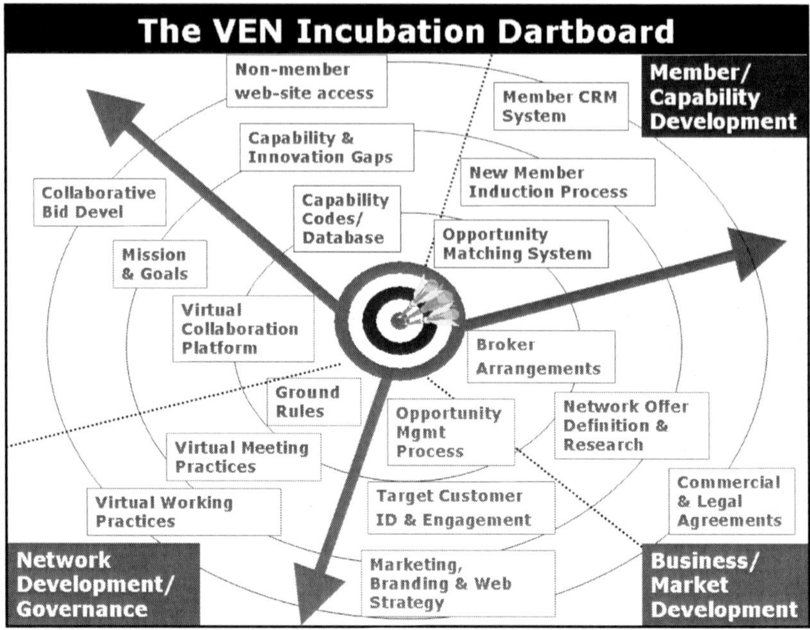

Initially, the ETC network was incubated using two main bioteaming techniques:

- Predator-Parasite (Ground Rules)
- Metabolism (Team Karma)

Technique#1: Predator-Parasite (Ground Rules)

This technique allowed the members to agree to a Yellow Card/ Red Card System. Yellow Card issues were situations, where if a certain thing happened (or did not happen), then trust would be damaged but it was recoverable. Red Card issues were situations, where trust would be broken in a way which was not recoverable, and the offending member would have to leave.

For example, providing inaccurate commercial information or bidding secretly against the network, were both seen as Red Card offences. Missing meetings without first sending an apology, or missing an internal (non-customer) project deadline, were agreed to be Yellow Card offences.

Technique#2: Metabolism (Team Karma)

This technique was used to identify what the members wanted

out of the network.

	Imp.	**Extent Achieved**	**How Long (months)**
1. Securing the networks' first collaborative contract	1.7	0.4	4.8
2. Feeling there are now excellent future prospects for winning new contracts (but not a specific sale yet)	1.6	1.1	3.9
3. Developing trust and strong relationships with other members	1.9	1.4	4.0
4. Access to new products, technologies and raw materials	1.4	0.6	5.8
5. Access to new suppliers	1.2	0.5	5.9

However, when we came to establish whether the members were prepared to play the necessary team roles to make this happen, the results were startling!

This is illustrated in the fragment of the Team Metabolism, shown overleaf below, on the critical area of Business/Market Development. This technique identified major leadership/team player gaps (the red sections), in a number of key areas that had to be addressed, before the network could move forward.

	Lead Take Resp.	Actively Participate	Contribute
B1 Bring Opportunities to Network – from existing contacts	0	7	7
B2 Bring Opportunities to Network – not existing contacts (e.g. cold call, tender scanning..)	1	2	10
B3 Ensuring all potential tender opportunities are properly investigated to closure or bid	2	5	6
B5 Prepare and conduct network sales presentations	0	3	8

In addition to this, there were three other bioteaming principles that the network adopted at its core:

Rule#7: Swarm! In a VEN all members are senior staff, within small autonomous businesses. They are totally independent of each other, so the environment does not lend itself to "command and control." Nobody can issue orders (and expect them to be followed!).

The network developed a set of key roles, easily remembered as "ABCDE," and shown below. This needed to be filled in a self-managing way for the network to flourish.

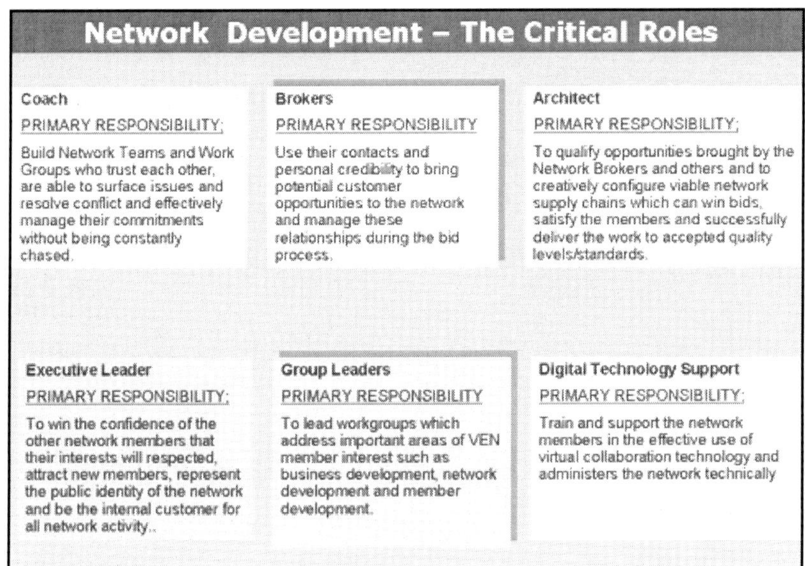

In addition, there were a small set of key behaviors that were agreed, and must be exhibited by every member such as "Every member a broker."

Rule 4: Always On! Leaders of small businesses spend lots of their time on the road, and may only check their emails in the evening (if at all). The only sure way to reach them is by mobile phone.

The team put in place a team message board to allow the leaders of the network to reach each member instantly by SMS, where required. This was invaluable, particularly for scheduling meetings as all replies were also stored on the message board.

Messenger > EX0006996 (447786209118) > Inbox English Español

Accounts | Inbox | Compose | Template | Contacts | Sent messages | Options | Buy Credits Delete | Download

From	Message	Received At
Tony Rooney	I will be there on 10th. TonyR	29/04/2005 12:14
ken	Yes	28/04/2005 14:07
ken	Yes	28/04/2005 14:07
dermot o'doherty	Will be there. dermot	28/04/2005 13:11
victor jordan	No sorry already committed.	28/04/2005 12:36
Peter Mee	Yes	28/04/2005 12:34
seamus mcquaid	Yes will be attending Seamus mc Quaid	28/04/2005 12:32
Felix O'Callaghan	Yes	28/04/2005 12:30
maria	Yes	28/04/2005 12:30
declan mooney	Book 2 seats for A.C.T.	28/04/2005 12:30

Rule 11: Porous Membranes: One of the problems of networks is that, when they become established, the existing members are often less than enthusiastic about recruiting new members. They feel this way for a number of reasons:

- more snouts in the trough
- worry about 'bad apple' members
- new members require induction and buddying, and slow the network down

However, one of the realities of networks is that members come and go and if you are not constantly recruiting new members, then the network will eventually shrivel up and die. Like any other living system, a network is either growing or dying, there is no in-between state.

The members found the porous membrane concept very useful. They agreed with the principle that the ETC should be "open enough to let good stuff in, but closed enough to keep bad stuff out."

This was translated into the ground rules, where all members agreed with the importance of, "Every member a recruiter," but with the proviso that the team had to formally agree to any new member joining.

The concept of Associate Member was also used to try prospective members out, before asking them to sign-up to the ground rules as full members.

5. Results Achieved

Tangibles:

- Award of a first collective contract
- Award of "Best Enterprise On-line Community"
- Joint bid for large-scale local waste management
- Establishment of marketing and business development groups
- Cross-Border Funding for Marketing Executive
- Public Marketing Website
- Comprehensive member handbook for collaborative working

Intangibles:

- External project associations and benefits

- Individual company business developments
- Extra-network links
- Commercial opportunities (company specific)

6. Lessons Learned:

The network first needed to develop a secure base, from which to build sustainable trust in the long term. This was achieved through development of open communications, rules of engagement and awareness of other member's needs and concerns.

The establishment of a shared IT and messaging platform, also allowed for continual communication and 'openness' between all client companies. This permitted all to share files and projects and thus, contributed to establishing the strong foundation necessary for the cluster to develop.

Through a planned series or workshops, conference calls and seminars, the team were able to develop a process allowing for the development of viable ground rules, the patient evolution of partners to undertake key leadership roles, and the development of short term and long-term goals/strategies.

Key to the success of the ETC venture was that the network was owned and driven by the member companies, with strong supporting external facilitation. This allowed the companies to maintain their individual visions, while ensuring the network developed in a strategic way, perceived as fair and equitable to all members.

7. Team Member Feedback

"ETC is a dynamic platform that has provided us with new business opportunities both nationally and internationally." – Seamus McQuaid, Eurofins Scientific Dundalk.

"ETC has become a powerful tool for collaborative effort whilst still allowing for individual gain!" – Des Durkan, AllClear.

"Being a member of ETC has allowed us to develop mutually beneficial partnerships with companies previously seen as competitors." – Stephen Sheppard, Norlect Engineering.

Daisyhill: Hospital Intermediate Care Team

1. The Bioteam

Daisyhill Hospital – Intermediate Care Team (ICT)

The Intermediate Care Team, is based at Archway within Newry and Mourne locality, part of Southern Health and Social Care Trust (Northern Ireland), comprising of 15 members of a multidisciplinary Team, including Physiotherapists, Occupational Therapists, Rehabilitation Workers, Social Workers, Clerical Officers and Intermediate Care Coordinator, who deliver rehabilitation services across the Newry and Mourne Locality to over 900 patients and clients per annum, in their own home or normal place of residence.

Each team member spends around 70% of his/her time away from the hospital, and relies heavily on mobile phones for coordination with base, and with other team members.

2. Background and Context

A mobile team such as the ICT face certain communication challenges that must be addressed using their mobile phones, rather than computer or web access: *One Knows – all know.*

The team needs to be kept informed instantly with important news, originating either from base or from another team member. For example, a team member finds out that a patient has died and needs to inform the rest of the team. Another example is, when a team member encounters road works or a traffic jam that would impact on the other members.

Ask the network: There needs to be a way for base, or another team member, to make an urgent request to the rest of the team. For example, a team member is delayed by traffic, and he/she needs to know if somebody else is closer to Mr. Smith, and could reach them first.

Its better "not" to talk: Voice calls are a very expensive and ineffective way to coordinate this kind of team. This is because, voice is really a 1:1 mechanism and if you want to contact "n" people you must make "n" phone calls. This is exacerbated by Newry's unique border location, which means that mobile phone calls are constantly dropping or switching to the international network that results in extra costs due to "roaming charges."

3. Objectives

The primary objective was to improve multi-disciplinary team communication/collaboration, by achieving:

- Instant access to all members of team, despite location.
- The ability to send messages to smaller geographically based teams.
- Reduction in effort when the same message is to be communicated to more than one member of the team.
- A Potential cost savings in relation to mobile calls to team members.
- Resolution of health and safety issues, in relation to accessing calls on the move.
- Support for facilitation of discharge, and prevention of hospital admission, as this opens up communication.
- A reduction in effort in contacting team members as a result of network issues in certain areas.
- The ability for teams to directly communicate with each other in relation to message received.
- The freeing up of an administration officer to carry out other duties.

The project was financially supported by *The Office of The First and Deputy First Minister for Northern Ireland* (OFMDFMNI).

4. How bioteaming was used

To achieve these objectives, the ICT team employed two key bioteaming principles – Always On! and Team Intelligence.

Rule#4: Always On! The team adopted *Swarmteams*, a group messaging tool that is based on the bioteaming principles, as the mechanism for keeping each team member continuously connected.:

- Each member of the team was invited to join a "Swarm" via text message.
- Each day urgent messages would be communicated to the team via a Swarm Broadcast that would go to all team members, as texts to their mobile phones.

These Swarm Broadcasts could be via the web or via any team member's mobile phone.

All broadcast messages were also stored on a web message-board along with any replies from team members.

Rule#2: Team Intelligence: Team Intelligence is about making sure that urgent information is communicated immediately to all team members, on their preferred device (in this case, mobile phones).

The Swarmteams tool assigns a purpose to each of its messages that neatly reflect the 6 main uses of mobile team communications:

Message Type	**Reply Expected**	**Purpose**
Info-Announce	NO	Internal announcements
Info-Newsflash	NO	External announcements
Request-Feedback	YES	Request for feedback (e.g. on a document)
Request-Poll	YES	Request for your vote
Request-Question	YES	Request for information/help
Request-Schedule	YES	Request availability for a meeting

5. Results Achieved

The bioteaming approach resulted in a number of concrete and specific benefits to the ICT team including:

- The Intermediate Care Team did not have to interrupt provision of patient care to receive potentially urgent telephone calls, as these came in via text message instead.
- Better referral management: new referrals could be seen within 0 - 24 hours of referral.
- Improved coordination of multidisciplinary teams, working with instant access to all members of team, despite location.
- Improved clinical decision making: fieldwork teams were able to screen referrals, and agree to timely follow up from any location, within the Trust
- All "step up" client referrals were seen in their own home or place of residence, on the same day if required, as opposed to attending Hospital.
- Alerts confirming hospital discharge were forwarded to the fieldwork teams, to facilitate efficient caseload management.
- Field work teams were able to access and respond to messages left at base, as opposed to returning to base, to pick up telephone or Fax messages.
- Team members were able to respond to new referrals based on their current location, thus improving access to services for patients and saving travel miles for the team.
- Optimized use of central admin staff in managing messages.
- Major reduction in effort, when the same message had to be communicated to more than one member of the team.
- Health and Safety issues resolved in relation to accessing calls on the move.
- Reduction in effort involved in contacting team members, as a result of poor signal issues in certain areas.

6. Lessons Learned

Use of the bioteaming techniques has made the mobile ICT team much more effective in a number of ways. However, working like a bioteam is somewhat counter-intuitive to staff, who have spent all their working lives in centralized command and control teams supported exclusively by IT systems.

Extra training and support was required in two critical areas concerning the use of mobile phone text: *160 characters is enough.*

It is possible to get 95% of messages into the 160 characters with a bit of training and thought. Standard abbreviations can be developed and used (e.g., TTYL – Talk to you Later). The text message must either convey the critical information, or indicate to the receiver that they must check their email or the web for the full message. *Anyone can broadcast from their mobile phone – no computer required!*

Team members need to have it reinforced that they do not have to wait to get to a computer, before they can broadcast. Swarmteams offers three useful broadcast commands from the handset accessory that can be used by any team member:

- TELL – send a message to the whole team – don't need a reply
- ASK – send a message to the whole team – replies copied to senders phone
- CHAT – send a message to the whole team – replies copied to all member's phones

7. Team Member Feedback

"Intermediate Care offers a range of integrated services to prevent unnecessary hospital admission, promote faster recovery from illness, support timely discharge and maximize independent living.

"The success of the bioteams approach to mobile team working has been the overall positive impact it has made on the Intermediate Care Teams ability to deliver accessible and responsive patient care in the clients own home, enabling the right person to make the most appropriate decision at the right time." – Jacqueline Morton, Team Leader, Intermediate Care Team.

"Bioteaming has facilitated the Trust in supporting multidisciplinary teams to collaborate more seamlessly, by using a diverse range of electronic communications. This approach is enabling enhanced inter/intra team communications and directly contributes to the provision of safer and higher quality care for service users." – Stephen Powell, Communications and Technology Manager.

CTSL: Telecoms Industry Working Party

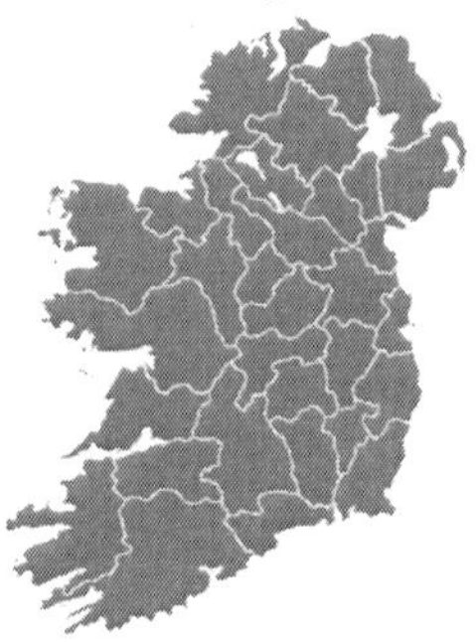

1. The Bioteam

The bioteam consisted of a number of key players from the telecoms and software industry in Ireland, who had come together to confirm the level of industry support for, and overall viability of, an all-island Convergent Telecoms Software Laboratory (CTSL).

The team included representatives from all the key stakeholders in the private sector including:

- Enterprise Development Agencies
- Software Associations including the Irish Software Association (ISA) and Momentum
- Software Companies
- Telecom Operators, including Vodafone and O2
- Systems Integrators, including Ericsson and Bell Labs
- Applied Research Groups, including the University of Ulster and the TSSG (Waterford)

2. Background and Context

It became clear at the outset that this team was not a typical, operationally focused team. Jon Katzenbach and Douglas Smith, in an article *The Discipline of Teams*, published in the *Harvard Business Review* identified three broad types of teams:

- *Recommender Teams:* those that recommend things – task forces or project groups
- *Doer Teams:* those that make or do things – manufacturing, operations, or marketing groups
- *Managing Teams:* those that run things – groups that oversee some significant functional activity

It was clear that the CTSL was closest in profile to a Recommender Team, but it was in fact a hybrid team – 70% a Recommender Team and 30% a Managing Team.

As a result, it faced three very specific challenges common to these kinds of teams:

1. *Time/Scheduling:* The team members are all senior industry players, and the one thing they don't have is time. Meetings are very difficult to schedule, and each meeting must be very well organized to ensure the essential items are covered. If this is not done well, the team will be unable to do the necessary work between meetings.
2. *Lack of a "Document Engine:"* There is no shortage of people who are able to review documents and presentations, but typically no-one on the team has the time to do any of these, in the first place. A team like this needs the support of a facilitator and a project manager. The CTSL is a team where membership is totally voluntary and made up of senior players, who have very limited ability, or desire, to do detailed work between team meetings.
3. *Consensus Building:* The CTSL includes representatives from all the main stakeholders, each of whom bring a different perspective on what is required. Within each stakeholder group there are multiple participants, each one representing different companies, each of whom have their own specific commercial interests.

Seeking to find a viable consensus is the biggest challenge for a team like this.

3. Objectives

To confirm the level of industry support for, and overall viability of, an all-island Convergent Telecoms Software Laboratory (CTSL), based on the initial government-sponsored feasibility study developed by consultants, and provide sufficient support and viability options, develop a Strategic Action Plan in partnership with all the relevant stakeholders.

The project was supported by *InterTradeIreland* the Trade Development Body.

4. How bioteaming was used

In planning the execution of the assignment, it was identified immediately that a critical success factor would be, to find a way to engage effectively with the key commercial stakeholders, to determine if there was real industry demand for a CTSL.

The consequence of not gaining real engagement with these commercial stakeholders would be, a strategic action plan that would look good on paper, but lack substance as it would not have any real commitment, or a sense of shared investment with the industry.

Industry might well "sign-up" to such a plan (as it would cost them nothing to do so), in the hope that it might be funded by the government. However, this would not provide a viable foundation for establishing an all-island Convergent Telecoms Software Laboratory with a strong chance of success and sustainability. Therefore, at an initial planning workshop involving the team sponsors, we designed the teams engagement approach as follows:

- Develop a Common Statement of Purpose
- Design and resource viable sub-groups for developing more detailed work plans

Using the Metabolism Technique (T3) to develop a Common Statement of Purpose

First, we designed a set of questions to be used in a one-hour 1:1 telephone interview with each of the stakeholder participants, to try and establish what each stakeholder group wanted out of the project, and equally importantly, what they were prepared to put in.

CTSL – Metabolism Questions

Once we conducted each of the interviews, we consolidated them together and presented them back to the entire group (see figure overleaf for a summary). The purpose of this was to sanity check whether the idea of the CTSL made sense to each set of stakeholders, both individually and collectively:

- Did they all want something that was broadly coherent?
- Was it important enough to all of them, and who was it the most important to (these parties would be more likely to be

willing to play active leadership roles)?

- What was each party prepared to put in, and did it leave any "big holes" that could not be filled in some way?

Fortunately, the answers to all these questions were sufficient for the team to continue, but this was by no means a foregone conclusion.

Stakeholder Group	**Software & Media Companies**	**Telecoms Operators**	**Systems Integrators & Equipment Suppliers**
1. What do they really want to get from the WTL?	A. Access to affordable, neutral, telecoms network testing and certification facilities. B. Enhance development of telecoms and creative clusters C. Create showcase location for sector	E. Strengthen and improve linkages and collaboration within sector to provide better (faster) product flow through earlier visibility and taking the operator off the critical path	F. Enhance value of existing commercial test facilities and research. G. Create efficiencies /benefits which could be shared down the entire SI supply chain.
2. How important is this to them? 1=MUST HAVE 2=SHOULD HAVE 3=NICE TO HAVE	A=1, B=2, C=2	E=2	F=3, G=2, C=2
3. What are they prepared to put in to get it?	1. USAGE FEES/M'SHIP	1. CAPITAL 2. SPONSORSHIP 3. USAGE FEES & M'SHIP	1. H/W & S/W FACILITIES & STAFF 2. USAGE FEES & M'SHIP 3. JOINT PROJECTS & MARKETING 4. MGMT & DIRECTION

CTSL – Consolidated Team Metabolism: Using the Cell Division Technique (T7) to create *viable sub-groups to develop detailed work plans.* A number of things became very clear from the outset:

- The whole team would only be able to meet occasionally, and these meetings would not be effective forums for getting detailed work done.
- Detailed work would have to be produced in smaller sub-groups.

It would not be possible to allocate individuals to sub-groups, based on what the sponsors thought. To get the individual's commitment it would be necessary for the individuals to "volunteer" for the sub-groups they wished to participate in. We identified three key sub-groups:

1. Work Group 1 – Business Model and Funding
2. Work Group 2 – Operations and Technology
3. Work Group 3 – Implementation and Launch

To achieve these objectives the ICT team embodied two key bioteaming principles – Stop Controlling and Self-Organizing Networks.

Rule#1: Stop Controlling

This was never going to be a team that could be led through a "command and control" approach. To try to do so would not work, and would also be massively frustrating for all parties, a classic example of trying to "herd cats."

With a team such as this, it is necessary to agree to a broad objective (in this case the Common Statement of Purpose), simple Ground rules (see my Predator-Parasite Technique), and then to identify and resource a small set of sub-groups. Then just step back, encourage and support, and let them get on with it!

Groups like this cannot be controlled or managed. Just like biological organisms they can only be perturbed, catalyzed, guided and encouraged. Similarly, their progress and outcomes are not totally predictable.

Rule#10: Self-Organizing Networks

A bioteam defines itself not in terms of its outputs, but in terms of its "network transformations." The original output defined for this team was to produce an action plan.

However, the team was not ready or resourced to produce such a plan. The traditional approach would have been to have them produce it anyway, and hope that somebody else would pick it up later and breathe life into it.

The bioteaming approach recognizes that unless the conditions are right, specific team outputs are not worth the paper they are written on.

Thus, the CTSL focused on the *pre-conditions* for success:

1. Understanding what motivated each team member, and trying to form a "collective encompassing goal."
2. Using 'collective leadership' techniques to identify the right leaders for the right sub-task, and letting them get on with it (within broad boundaries).

Once these two pre-conditions were in place it became possible to produce an action plan, but not within this project timeline or set of resources!

5. Results Achieved

Tangibles: As a team, the CTSL, in collaboration with the commercial stakeholders, developed a Common Statement of Purpose document, plus Terms of References for three Work Groups to develop the details:

- Work Group 1 – Business Model and Funding
- Work Group 2 – Operations and Technology
- Work Group 3 – Implementation and Launch

Intangibles: In a sense, the most important results from this project were not the specific deliverables above, but the creation of a powerful network of people, all committed to the development of the Convergent Software Industry in Ireland. The key enablers of this network were Trust, Consensus and Enthusiasm.

The value of this network was demonstrated by a subsequent major collaboration between a number of the CTSL players, in forming the SDP Alliance (www.thesdpalliance.com), a collaboration of Irish telecoms software product companies, all established leading vendors of category-defining products:

- Aepona
- Changing Worlds
- Cibenix
- Mobile Cohesion
- Openet
- Xiam

Because of market feedback, they realized that a major CSF towards offering a cost effective, customized, end-to-end Service Delivery Platform (SDP) to the market, would be a close collaboration of best of breed products, that are pre-integrated with internal and external enablers.

6. Lessons Learned

Denis Murphy from Mobile Cohesion and Industry, Chairperson of the initiative, deals honestly with the harsh reality of these kinds of teams: "The Key lesson learned is that initiatives like this need to be of commercial focus, or need to be strategic to the participants. We are all very busy senior level people in the industry. This was a "nice to do," but not critical or strategic to our businesses. Hence we did not have a lot of time to devote to it."

Denis then underscores the point that sometimes the right thing to do is *not* to deliver the objectives the team has been set: "For me, the most important thing to come out of this was the network and the trust between members. The relationships and thinking that happened as part of this process led to the development of the SDP Alliance, which was more commercially focused, and hence was something that members would spend more time on."

To produce this kind of consensus as opposed to token consensus, requires a huge amount of effort and openness on the part of team members, but this replays itself many times over in the quality of the subsequent collaboration.

This project shows very clearly that "Recommender Teams" cannot be managed by traditional team management techniques.

7. Team Member Feedback

Denis Murphy from Mobile Cohesion and Chairperson of the initiative sums it up: "I think the process was excellent, particularly the 1:1 interviews. This allowed the sub-groups to be assembled even before the formal meeting."

8. Sample Terms of Reference for a Bioteam Work Group

A. Work Group Name, WG1 – Business Model and Funding

B. Work Group Leader – e.g., Denis Murphy

C. Core Work Group Members – (name at least three)

D. Main Work Group Deliverable – e.g.,

1. To take the Common Statement of Purpose for the CTSL, and develop from it a business model covering a five-year period, and showing projected capital requirements, operating costs and projected revenues.

2. It should also identify all possible sources of all capital and on-going funds, including the possibility of direct (e.g., cash) funding, in-kind funding (e.g., equipment, access and expertise), sponsorships, subscriptions and commissions.

3. It should demonstrate the creation of measurable value of CTSL for all stakeholders for the life of the initiative – for example, in the form of the accelerated pace of growth of participating companies, total people employed in the sector, a reduction in time to market for new products, companies achieving breakthrough to T1 Operator supplier status, and Intellectual Property value.

We should specify the main types of stakeholder (from small software company to telecoms OpCo), and describe the unique engagement process of each type with the CTSL, and their engagement with each other.

E. Deliverable Contents/Structure

Business Model Executive Summary (Suggest maximum of five pages) A short narrative that summarizes the key numbers, elements, assumptions and critical success factors within the business model, including, but not restricted to the profile of the existing and intended competitive positions of the wireless industry sector and associated stakeholders. We should distinguish the roles, responsibilities and anticipated benefits for the major stakeholder groups, accepting that this initiative is aimed at increasing the competitive performance of companies in the wireless software sector in particular, and also through its influence and effect, the competitive performance of other areas of the Convergent Telecommunications sector.

Business Model Spreadsheet (and supporting narrative).
Showing the following costs and revenues over the agreed five-year period:

1. *Capital Requirements* – Buildings, Technology and other Infrastructure, including the demonstrator facilities.
2. *On-going Costs* – Operational Management, Hardware and Software Platform updates, and Sales & Marketing
3. *Governance costs* – cost of managing the participation of funders, beneficiary companies, industry bodies and enterprise agencies in the form of a Steering/Management Committee.
4. *On-going Revenue Streams* – split down by the different sources, including the possibility of direct cash funding, and in-kind funding, e.g., equipment and expertise, sponsorships, subscriptions and commissions, with assumptions defined.
5. The total level of funding that will be required (both cash funding and in-kind funding), from all sources.

F. Other Key Parties/Relevant Initiatives

What other individuals will be liaised, or invited to participate in review outputs, from this working group to ensure it properly takes into account other relevant initiatives?

- Private Sector – Other Wireless initiatives as identified in the previous report.
- Public Sector – National and Regional Enterprise policy actors on both sides of the border.

G. Delivery Timetable

Milestone/Output By When:

1. TR/Plan/Leader/Core members approach agreed to and Draft#1 Circulated to rest of CTSL stakeholder group

2. Draft#2 Incorporating CTSL stakeholder comments and released for external comment
3. Draft#3 Incorporating external comments

H. Working Approach

The work group intends to organize its work as follows:

- Background information gathering
- Ideas generation/direction setting
- Liaising with other groups/external parties
- Detailed drafting/word-smithing
- Managing the deliverable review process

I. Other Important Considerations

1. This work group needs to liaise with the other two work groups.
2. There is a need to identify a major source of funding at an early stage.
3. This work group also needs to address the following team review comments:
   (Developing Elevator Pitch(es))
   (Context/Positioning regarding Other Initiatives)

DK: Conference Organization

1. The Bioteam

Dynamic Knowledge – Conference Organizers

During November 2006, Dynamic Knowledge (www.dynamic-knowledge.com), a leading London-based performance and learning consulting company, organized two one-day, back-to-back, workshops on key leadership, performance and learning topics impacting employers today; under the banner – Leadership & Performance Futures 2006.

These workshops were aimed at senior HR and learning and development professionals like, Training Managers/Directors, CEOs, and HR Managers/Directors.

It was planned that both workshops would be facilitated by, and participative with, input from leading industry practitioners and analysts, and with attendance at each limited to just 80 delegates each day, to enable maximum interaction and dialogue.

2. Background and Context

These days, conference organizers face a number of serious challenges, in particular:

- Getting potential delegates' attention, given all the other competition for their time.
- Finding effective ways to invite people, given the lack of effectiveness of email as a channel.
- Minimizing no-shows. Even if delegates have paid, those that don't show up reduce the networking potential and event usefulness for the other delegates.

- Getting broad and active participation at the event, not just with a small set of highly vocal individuals.
- Finding a way to continue some form of interaction between delegates, after the event ends.

3. Objectives

DK Director, and overall conference sponsor, Debbie Carlton decided to take a radically different approach to the event, based on the bioteaming model and specifically:

1. Use of "Word of Mouth" invitations, as a major means of attracting a good mix of delegates.
2. Build up "buzz" before the event, by constant, relevant communications using multiple channels like email, web and mobile phones.
3. Enable and encourage enhanced delegate participation at the event, using mobile devices and laptops.

4. How bioteaming was used

To achieve these objectives, the DK team designed the event around three key bioteaming principles – Symbiosis, Clustering and Always-On.

Rule#5: Symbiosis

By Symbiosis bioteams fully include all parties, whether they be customers or suppliers, as full and trusted partners in the team.

Normally, when you think about a conference, you think about the organizers as the team. The delegates are seen as the customers, and the external speakers as the suppliers, neither of which are considered part of the team.

However, the consequence of this thinking is that you are not able to take full advantage of the networks of the customers and speakers, in attracting the best possible audience to the event.

So it was decided right from the onset, that there would be one team that would include the most committed delegates and the speakers, as well as the DK staff.

Rule#6: Cluster

The decision to have one team, laid the foundations for the

second bioteaming principle, Cluster. In bioteaming, this means using the natural relationship of the whole team as the best way to engage with the rest of the community.

To make this work, the Team Ties technique (T6) was used to identify the key connectors, who could be used as the engines of word-of-mouth marketing to the rest of the potential delegates.

The key criteria was to find past delegates who were:

a) enthusiastic about the topic
b) well regarded and connected in their networks
c) could be relied on to invite others

Rule#4: Always On

The DK supported the event using *Swarmteams*, a group messaging tool that is based on the bioteaming principles. This acted as the final key enabler of Debbie's other two key event objectives:

- Building up buzz before the event by constant relevant communications, using multiple channels like email, web and mobile phones.
- Enabling and encouraging enhanced delegate participation at the event using mobile devices and laptops.

Each delegate received a small number of messages to build up their anticipation of the event, and to act as a reminder on the day before. At the event, the delegates were given some simple hands-on training in swarmteams and then encouraged to respond to speaker questions via their mobile phones or their wireless laptops. All messages and replies were stored on a web messageboard for the event that was projected on a large screen during the event and updated in real-time.

Swarmteams made it easy for delegates to give both attributed and anonymous feedback on event topics. Also it was possible for the speaker to analyze the results to questions in real time (see example below).

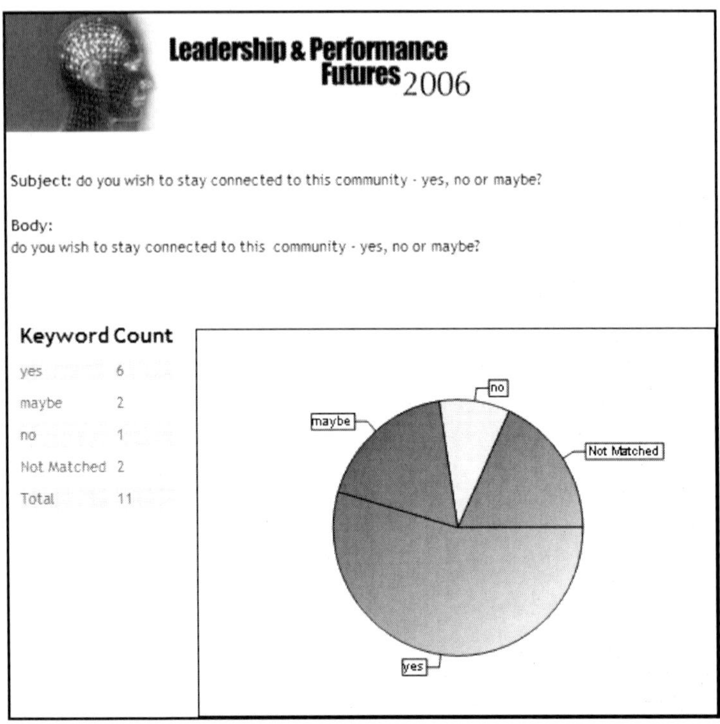

5. Results Achieved

The bioteaming approach resulted in a number of concrete and specific benefits to Leadership & Performance Futures 2006:

Tangibles:

- An event that used technology that recognizes the communication and engagement challenges; that is looking to minimize effort but increase effective dialogue.
- Useful capability for audience of 80, where organizers do not have time to be sure attendees are engaged and getting value.

Intangibles:

- Greater understanding of typical behavior of attendees (e.g., passive, until they choose to be active), derived from previous experience of large events and conferences.
- Allowed organizers to have more dialogue with attendees and gain early feedback that is actionable.

6. Lessons Learned

Debbie sums up the lessons learned: "Use of the bioteaming

approach created lots of new possibilities and energy round the event, and we will definitely use it again." With hindsight there are some things we learned for next time:

1. The Audience need to be very carefully engaged. It's easy to over-estimate the average person's initial reluctance to participate in an event, and who are unfamiliar with being offered a choice of communication/engagement channels or using the "tools" they have in events.
2. You need to send some fun messages first, so people can try the thing out and make mistakes without any possibility of them being embarrassed.
3. You really need to support each speaker with a facilitator who fully understands the technology, if you wish to do real-time feedback. It's hard for a single person to play both roles.
4. You need to have time to plan the use of this capability, to support the full lifecycle of event management. It's not something you can just do "on the fly."
5. You need to be clear how you will use the capability to support post-event dialogue, without being invasive.

7. Team Member Feedback

"The inclusion of the bioteams' approach to support the conference was a pilot engagement, and there was limited time to learn and apply the capability to its full potential. However, once certain foundational principles were understood, the set-up and use was easy.

"The event's audience were typically in the age range of 35-55, and users of various communication tools were not used to multitasking, or switching between channels, or using the tools they have during an event. They were more used to passive than active interaction at events.

"Bioteaming supported by real-time messaging is definitely a capability that should be used to support events that really want to enable dialogue and dynamic feedback. However, there is a need to expend effort in planning and initial engagement of all users to maximize its potential." – Debbie Carlton, Director, DK.

Lancelot: Virtual Language School

1. The Bioteam

LANCELOT School GmbH is a training center and job portal for live online language trainers.

2. Background and Context

Live online language training is a new profession. Language trainers meet their language students in virtual classrooms, to conduct highly interactive lessons using modern Internet communication technology. We are at the very beginning of the recognition of the possibilities of this new way of learning languages. In the minds of potential clients, this means timing in bringing this to market has to be just right.

On the background of a seemingly huge potential market, it seemed puzzling that a small team of language teachers were more than reluctant to register on the portal, which when first inaugurated was called www.letsteachonline.com.

A virtual team of live online language trainers presenting their offer via a single portal seemed to offer a powerful value offer to the market. As a team we would develop buying power for the technology and advertise this still new language training. However, a strong sense of competition between the language teachers brought the project virtually to a standstill, within weeks of it being launched.

This quarrelling came to a head around negotiating EU funding for developing a certified training course. The European Commission funded project LANCELOT, was eventually granted and development work commenced for a 2-year project involving 23 partners in 8 countries. In September 2007 the European project was finished successfully.

Yet, the problem of competition still existed. Team members were largely connected via Instant Messenger and regular team meetings and live online events were undertaken. Participation by core team members was very low. Commitment by core team members was also low.

3. Objectives

The specific objective for the participating companies was to strengthen their ability to compete on a global commercial stage, by creating a critical mass to enable the member companies to realize collective strength and individual potential, particularly through collective tendering, joint marketing, joint purchasing and joint R&D.

It was intended that the companies (as well as operating their normal business activities) should come together to define and construct a joint collaborative offer to the market. For example, a "one-stop-shop" or an innovative new bundling of resources such as increase in the number of languages on offer and the number of specialized language trainers.

4. How bioteaming was used

Bioteams Technique: Metabolism (Team Karma)

This technique was used to identify what the members wanted out of the collaboration.

PART1 - MEMBER EXPECTATIONS FROM NETWORK	Importance		
1. More students (teaching languages and others)		7	
2. Earn money as train-the-trainer		5	
3. Earn money as a shareholder		3	
4. Developing trust and strong relationships with other members		5	
5. Recognition (Academic), certificate		7	
6. Strengthen one's own school		5	
7. Access to affordable and latest technology, improved software, customized software, payment systems		6	
8. Access to teaching material, methods, ideas, LMS, assessment methodology, exams, e-learning		6	
9. Access to new knowledge, learn anything, personal development		8	

However, when we came to establish whether the members were prepared to play the necessary team roles to make this happen, the results were startling. This is illustrated in the fragment of the Team Metabolism shown below, on the critical area of Business/Market Development. This technique identified major leadership/team player gaps in a number of key areas that had to be addressed before the network could move forward. A fragment of this is shown below.

The abundance of dark in the Leadership and Active Team Member columns shows very clearly, that the teams were not prepared to make the necessary personal investments in effort and collective leadership to realize their personal and collective goals.

PART2 - MEMBER INPUTS TO NETWORK

For each of the following activities:
Lead/Take Responsibility
Mark X here if you are able to lead or take responsibility for this network activity
Actively Participate
Mark X here if you are able to actively participate or play a full role in a network team engaged in this activity including additional workgroup meetings
Contribute
Mark X here if you are able to make some contribution to this activity depending on how busy you are
Otherwise leave the activity blank!

Activity	Lead L	Partipate P	Contribute C
S&M = Sales and Marketing	0	1	0
S&M: Skype, continue negotiating	0	0	0
S&M: cold calling (the hardest sale ever!!)	0	1	1
S&M: word of mouth from existing customers	0	1	2
S&M: to build a reputation of EU-level (scientific/linguistic=endorsement)	0	0	0
S&M: Demos of language lessons on LANCELOTschool	1	0	0
S&M: Advertisement on good sites	0	1	1
S&M: Country specific canvassing	1	2	0
S&M: List of prospects, CRM	0	1	0
	0	0	0
Public Relation	0	0	0
PR: To create a Vision/Mission/Value Proposition statement	0	0	0
PR: Representing LANCELOTschool at public events/ online events	0	0	2
PR: Public Relation Interviews, Newsletters, Magazines	1	1	0
PR: Event Management	0	0	0
PR: Radio Show, Podcasting	0	0	1
PR: Market Research	0	0	2
PR: Publish articles/ blogs so as to demonstrate our expertise	0	1	0
	0	0	0
Strategic Decisions	0	0	0
Decided on potential partners, such as do we want to cooperate with other language schools/ organisations etc.	0	5	0
Pricing structure: to decide on our pricing? wages for teachers? own pricing of your own school? lesson price on LANCELOTschool?	0	5	2

5. Results Achieved

The bioteaming approach resulted in a number of concrete and specific benefits to the Lancelot team including:

1. Common goals were established.
2. A set of critical tasks were identified with clear accountabilities.
3. The 'Lack of leadership' problem surfaced.
4. We were able to see that the venture would not be able to succeed in its current form much longer, saving all parties opportunity costs.
5. We were able to refocus the collaborative venture into an area (Network Marketing), where we felt much more confident it would succeed.

6. Lessons Learned

Heike Philp, Managing Director of LANCELOT, shares what the team learned. There are 3 critical dimensions in a network enterprise such as Lancelot:

1. Network Development/Governance
2. Member/Capability Development
3. Business/Market Development

To succeed we knew we needed to develop all three dimensions in parallel. We would simply not succeed if we developed one (or even two) of these, at the expense of the others. This, indeed, is what happened. We did not have the necessary resources to develop all three dimensions and the network started to fragment. Subsequently, we made the painful, but correct decision, to discontinue the collaboration within its current focus.

There was also one major strategic business decision that led to the fragmentation of the team, a management decision to not engage in end-user business.

The good news is that we have now been able to refocus our venture, so as not to compete with the local language schools, but rather, assisting them to supply the demand. In this scenario, the language trainer is directly employed, or works freelance for the language school.

We in turn supply the teacher with the technology that they use in the school. Therefore the trainer becomes the end-user. This makes sense again because LANCELOT School wants to establish itself as a training center for language teachers and does not aim to become one big global language school.

7. Team Member Feedback

Although this story might seem in many places like a failure, it was, in fact, a success. Sometimes, the right decision in team mobilization is for the team to walk away from a shared objective that is not achievable or profitable, and to find a new collective objective that is both!

Use of the bioteaming techniques helped us to identify that our team did not have the necessary alignment of goals, capabilities and commitments, to create a successful collaborative venture in the area we were aiming for at this time.

Although this was very painful to realize, we were able to identify it very early through the approach, and make the right decision that the time was not right for this venture, much sooner than we would have, if we had just "muddled on." So the major benefit was that we spotted a doomed venture much sooner than we would otherwise have, with a huge opportunity cost saving for all parties.

The bioteaming approach also enabled us to see what our strengths (and weaknesses) were, so that when the opportunity came along to refocus the business on a new and more viable opportunity, Network Marketing, we were able to realize it.

"Bioteaming has facilitated the LANCELOT School with a strategy for teambuilding that enabled the management to immediately see the weakness in its business plan. One year after the intensive teambuilding activities, this virtual team disintegrated and discontinued. A new plan of action was deployed: network marketing." – Heike Philp, Managing Director of LANCELOT School GmbH.

Kharma45: Music Fan Engagement

1. The Bioteam

Kharma45 – A Music Band and its fans

Kharma45, an exciting young UK band from Derry, on the Warner Brothers Label, used bioteaming to form a unique partnership with their top fans, to promote their new single "Where's Your Spirit Man."

2. Background and Context

It is well reported that the Music Industry worldwide is in crisis (e.g., The Cult of the Amateur by Andrew Keen. [51]) This is visible in number of ways, for example:

- For every legal (paid) download there are 40 illegal copies.
- CD Sales are significantly down due to the ending of the "vinyl replacement" era.
- There's an explosion of music available (the "Long Tail"), but individual artist volumes are low, with even the major stars not selling anything like the volumes of CDs they used to.

For the up-and-coming or independent musician or band, this creates a very difficult environment where the chance of them landing some kind of deal with one of the major labels is not what it used to be. This is simply the economic consequences of the shrinking revenues at the majors (such as Universal, Warner and EMI) that make them reluctant to invest in new talent, as they seek less risky ways to make money. For example, the current industry focus on exploiting and licensing existing portfolios over new channels to market, rather than commissioning new talent.

So, the "catch-22" is that if the independent musician can show success, then they have a much better chance of a deal with a label. But, it is very challenging to reach this level of success without the backing of a label in the first place! So if an independent musician is to "succeed," then they probably will have to do it without the backing of a major label. Their success will depend on the ability and commitment of the musician/band (and their "management," to the extent such exists), to grow and manage a viable and passionate fan base that they can use to publicize/sell their music/merchandise, to recruit other fans, and to promote live activity .

In recognition of this problem, *NESTA* (The National Endowment for Science, Technology and the Arts), with the backing of a number of music labels, generously agreed to sponsor a selected number of UK bands and musicians to use Swarmteams (a multichannel community engagement system, based on biological principles) for free, for up to 12 months. Kharma45 was the first UK band to be accepted into the NESTA program!

3. Objectives

Johnny Davis, Kharma45 Band Manager, decided to take a radically different approach to fan engagement, using the bioteaming model and Swarmteams (www.swarmteams.com). The goal was to enhance Kharma45's existing social network strategies, based on popular sites such as Facebook (www.facebook.com) and Bebo (www.bebo.com), to fully include mobile devices and to make it more cost-effective:

1. Extend the Kharma45 fan base (The 'Kharma Army')
2. Create more dedicated and hard-working "superfans"
3. Create more 'buzz' around live and promotional events
4. Electronically sell new music tracks and merchandise through embedded e-commerce links in the messages

4. How bioteaming was used

Kharma45 centered their fan engagement strategy on three key bioteaming principles – Symbiosis, Clustering and Always-On.

Rule#5: Symbiosis

By Symbiosis, bioteams fully include all parties, whether they are customers or suppliers, as full and trusted partners in the team. When you think of a music band using the bioteaming approach, you automatically include their fans as part of the team. That way you are able to take full advantage of the fans' networks of relationships.

So it was decided right from the onset that there would be one Kharma45 bioteam that would include their fans as well as the band members. In Swarmteams terms, this translates into one Kharma45 "Swarm Community" consisting of multiple Swarms owned by band members and top fans.

The evolution of the Kharma45 Swarm Community is summarized in the diagram below that shows how the community evolved through the five stages in its development.

Swarm Maturity Model

	LEVEL	Main Characteristic
1	Mobilising	Core Team trained, roles & goals agreed
2	Core Swarm Ready	Community Owner and Team live
3	VIP Swarm Live	X Alpha members joined and trained
4	Alpha Swarms Live	X Alpha swarms live with Y Members
5	Community Buzzing	Z messages sent, forward and engaged

A key aspect of the Kharma45 strategy was, instead of broadcasting key messages to the entire fan base, to broadcast only to the Swarm of top fans in the VIP Swarm. Then these VIP fans would forward these messages to their own swarms with personal comments. This produced a much higher sense of intimacy for all messages and significantly improved open rates and click through. Message quality was maintained by a message ranking system, where the Alpha fans digital reputation would be impacted by whether the message recipients liked what they were being sent or not!

Rule#6: Cluster

The decision to have one Kharma45 team laid the foundations for the second bioteaming principle, Cluster. In bioteaming, this means using the natural relationships of the whole team as the best way to engage with the rest of the community.

To make this work, the band members identified the key connectors, the Alpha Fans, who could be used as the engines of word-of-mouth marketing to the rest of the fan base. (For more on this see the Team Ties technique).

Johnny Davis, Kharma45 Manager, explains the compelling mathematics, "I call our initial strategy 25^2 – imagine you can identify and take care of just 25 alpha fans really well. Then you encourage, and equip, and reward each of these 25 to take care of 25 other fans equally well. So you reach 625 fans. But if you do it properly, you don't have to worry about looking after the whole 625 fans, just the 25, that's just 4% of the fan base. And this is just Phase 1 – the real prize for us is 25^3 – to reach 15,625 fans (625 * 25) and still only worry about looking after the 25 – that's just 0.16% of the fan base!"

Rule#4: Always On

Kharma45 has a fan base, like many other bands, in the 15-35 demographic. For this demographic the preferred channel is mobile phone text message during the day, and instant message during the evening.

The band was able to stay in constant touch with the fans using Swarmteams' 'smart messaging' facility that first checks if a message recipient is online, and if so pings them an instant message. If it does not find them online, only then does it send them a text.

5. Results Achieved

The project has only been running for a couple of months, but the bioteaming approach has already resulted in a number of concrete and specific benefits for Kharma45 including:

- The active partnership and support of 25 Alpha Fans
- Over 500 fans signed up in a matter of a few weeks by these Alpha Fans
- An *instant hotline* to all known Kharma45 fans to promote new tracks, concerts, special events and band news at a single click
- A way to identify and reward the most dedicated fans
- Much higher open rates and response rates than other

approaches to fan engagement
- A way to differentiate the band by using Open Swarms to recruit new members via their existing online profiles in *Facebook, Myspace,* blogs and the web

6. Lessons Learned

Johnny summed up the main lessons learned:
- First, you need to take care of the social aspects of bioteaming. If you just send out a message to someone's mobile phone there is about a one in ten chance they will act on it. So, what we did first was to have the actual band members call their small select group of superfans to sell them the benefits of joining the VIP Swarm, and to tell them to expect a message to follow in a minute. This way we got nearly a 100% sign-up!
- Second, you need to make the Alpha Fans feel special – we put a huge amount of effort into recognition and rewards and this really paid off.
- Third, you need to be flexible – you try a type of message or some link or some promotion and it does not work, so you change it a bit and try again. If it works then you put more resources into it, if it does not work you put your resources elsewhere. That's the way nature works – I think the technical term is a "Genetic Algorithm." (See Bioteams Rule 9 for more).

7. Team Member Feedback

According to lead Vocalist, *Glenn Rosborough*, bioteaming worked for the fans: "It's now big kudos to be a Kharma45 Alpha Fan because you also get to distribute this information to others, and are rewarded for signing up new fans. So it was a great way to increase our fan base and also to let them feel more involved with the band."

Peter Doherty (lead guitar) thought the bioteams approach worked for the band too: "As well as showing our top fans how much we appreciate them, Swarmteams gives us an instant, mobile SMS channel for promoting our music and concerts."

Part 7: Future directions in bioteams

26. Biocrowds – the next evolution

Could a virtual team have a million members? Recent developments in mass collaboration, distributed computing and the wisdom of crowds suggest, the answer might be yes.

Mass Collaboration and Virtual Crowds

One of the differences between human teams and some biological teams is *sheer scale in terms of number of members.*

Human teams rarely exceed fifty and a typical large single human organization might contain ten thousand members. Human organizations much bigger than this obviously exist, but they tend to organize themselves into smaller independently managed sub-units.

However, biological teams such as Ant or Bee societies, can contain *up to a million members in a single mature colony* or hive – all of whom can act as a unit.

Up until recently, this has meant that some dimensions of biological teamwork and group behavior were not able to be reproduced in human teams and organizations due to this lack of scale.

The Internet might change all this.

A June 20, 2005 *Newsweek* magazine article, "The Power of Us," [52] reports that "Mass Collaboration on The Internet is shaking up Business." The article identifies three types of Internet-based "mass collaboration" that I would characterize as:

- *Give and Take* – for example creating shared, distributed computing capacity
- *Needles in Hay*stacks – connecting to other like-minds through shared interest, rather than personal relationship
- *Participation through Passion* – co-inventing with others based on

passion, rather than money as the motivator

What can nature's large-scale teams teach us about Internet-based Mass Collaboration?

- Are these initiatives significant?
- Are they the "leading edge" of very important new group social practices?
- Are they merely a number of novel ventures conveniently grouped together under the topical buzz-phrase "Internet mass collaboration?"
- Do they represent "collaboration" or something else altogether?
- The effect of "scale" on collaboration?

"Scale" enables some particularly useful characteristics in nature's teams, such as:

- *Reduced vulnerability to individual member failure:* Individual member actions are unlikely to alter the overall group outcome due to the sheer numbers involved.
- *Swarm Intelligence:* Simple individual behaviors can produce amazingly sophisticated collective results. Examples of this include birds flocking, schools of fish and ants, and their amazing scheduling and routing capabilities.
- *Emergent Behavior:* Swarming and school formation is a known Emergent Behavior. An emergent behavior can appear when a number of simple entities (agents) operate in an environment, forming more complex behaviors as a collective. The property itself is often unpredictable and unprecedented, and represents a new level of the system's evolution. The complex behavior or properties are not a property of any single entity, nor can they easily be predicted or deduced from behavior in the lower-level entities.

Give and Take

Newsweek magazine featured Skype, the Voice over IP player, which at that stage had attracted over 40 million users and has changed the face of global telecoms industry. "When users fire up Skype, they automatically allow their spare computing power and connections to be borrowed by the Skype network that uses that collective resource to route others calls. This creates a self-sustaining phone system requiring no capital investment based on users spare capacity."

However, Skype is just one example of the power of *distributed or grid computing* that has already been exploited by a number of other non-commercial initiatives such as:

- *Search for Extraterrestrial Intelligence (SETI):* SETI@home is a scientific experiment that uses Internet-connected computers in the Search for Extraterrestrial Intelligence (SETI), by running a free program that downloads and analyzes radio telescope data.
- *Protein Folding:* Folding@Home is a distributed computing project that studies protein folding, mis-folding, aggregation, and related diseases. By using novel computational methods and large scale distributed computing, they have been able to simulate timescales thousands to millions of times longer than previously achieved.
- *World Community Grid:* World Community Grid's mission is to create the largest public computing grid benefiting humanity. IBM has donated the hardware, software, technical services and expertise to build the infrastructure for World Community Grid, and provides free hosting, maintenance and support.

Needles in Haystacks

The *Newsweek* article reports on the success of Innocentive Inc., a network of 80,000 independent self-selected problem solvers in 173 countries established by Eli Lilly & Co, but open to anyone to use. For example, Proctor & Gamble have achieved their objective of increasing external development of new products from 20% to 35% by using networks such as Innocentive as "ways of reaching independent talent." InnoCentive works like this:

- ✔ Major Pharma companies contract with InnoCentive in order to become "Seekers"
- ✔ They post "Challenges" to InnoCentive.com
- ✔ Each Challenge includes a detailed description and requirements, a deadline, and an award amount for the best solution

✔ Awards range from $10,000 to $100,000

InnoCentive is an example of how the reach of the Internet can be used to connect to like-minds on the basis of shared interest, rather than personal relationship.

Once the necessary critical scale is achieved, then the network can become self-sustaining. With increasing scale, challenges are more likely to be solved. This creates good publicity that attracts more seekers and more independent scientists into the network.

Participation through Passion

The whole Open Source Software movement (OSS) is probably the best known example of the innovative power of individuals, once they are provided with the opportunity to be creative in an area that stimulates them

The article reports on SugarCRM, a 10-person company developing an OSS Customer Relationship Management tool that has now been downloaded 250,000 times.

Equally interesting is the success of OhmyNews, a South Korean Online Newspaper involving 36,000 "citizen journalists" writing up to 200 stories per day.

The Demos Thinktank produced a very forward-thinking minibook [53], suggesting the wider community benefits possible in using OSS principles, in areas of community and government, well beyond the software development domain.

So what does "mass collaboration" really mean?

First, "mass collaboration" clearly has all the traits of an important new and emerging group – a new social practice, only made possible by the Internet. It would be foolish to try to ignore it.

Second, it is collaboration – but not as we know it.

In an earlier chapter, "Four Types of teamwork in a bioteam," I introduced the different types of teamwork in a biological team [41]:

- *Solowork* – members doing same things at different times
- *Crowdwork* – members doing the same thing at the same time
- *Groupwork* – members doing different things at different times (sequential)
- *Teamwork* – members doing different things at same time (concurrent)

The examples of mass collaboration we have seen so far are either Crowdwork (e.g., Skype and InnoCentive) or Groupwork (e.g., OSS and Citizen Journalism), but not Teamwork.

We have yet to see whether *mass virtual teamwork* is possible – or not?

Third, we won't be able to fully predict what happens next! One of the most interesting aspects of these phenomena is the fact, that they all demonstrate *emergent behavior,* which means we cannot predict exactly how they will evolve.

For example, Internet mass collaborations may evolve into even more valuable forms of mass collaboration, by starting to operate as networks (with connections between individual members). Today they operate more as star formations (with connections mostly between individual members and the center). Alternatively, it may turn out that some of the most advanced forms of collaboration are only available to small teams, and not accessible to teams of the size we are starting to see in Internet mass collaborations.

Chapter Summary

Biological teams, such as ant or bee societies, can contain *up to a million members in a single mature colony* or hive, all of whom can act as a unit. Up until recently, this has meant that some dimensions of biological teamwork and group behavior were not able to be reproduced in human teams and organizations due to this lack of scale.

However, the ability of the Internet to facilitate mass collaboration has led to new and potentially, hugely important types of teams based strongly on bioteam principles:

- *Give and Take* – for example creating shared distributed computing capacity
- *Needles in Hay*stacks – connecting to other like-minds through shared interest rather than personal relationship
- *Participation through Passion* – co-inventing with others based on passion rather than money as the motivator

Index – Not

Due to the nature of this book, we have provided an extensive table of contents to better serve the purpose of an index.

References

1. Frankl, Viktor E, *Man's search for meaning : an introduction to logotherapy*, Simon & Schuster, 1984.
2. Seligman, Martin.,. *Learned Optimism – How to change your mind and your life*, Free Press, 1990.
3. Clippinger, John Henry, *The Biology of Business – Decoding the Natural Laws of Enterprise*, Jossey-Bass, 1999.
4. Wessel, David, "Motivating Workers by giving them a vote," *Wall Street Journal Online*, August 2005.
5. Fishman, Charles, "Engines of Democracy," *Fast Company Magazine*, September 1999.
6. Gatz, Scott, "Trusting a community to get it right," *Scott Gatz's Blog*, February 2006.
7. Fryer, Peter, "An organization case study in complex adaptive systems," *www.bioteams.com*, July 2005.
8. Carson, Scott , "Boeing Celebrates the Premiere of the 787 Dreamliner," *Boeing Corporation* News Release, July 2007.
9. Introna, Lucas, Hope Moore and Cushman, Mike "The Virtual Organization – Technical or Social Innovation? Lessons from the Film Industry," *London School of Economics*, Working Paper Series, No. 72, 1999.
10. Teeman, Brian, "Roles and responsibilities of users and community members in an open source project," *www.MamboServer.com*, 2005.
11. Rheingold, Howard, *Smart mobs: the next social revolution*, Perseus Pub., 2003.

12. Good, Robin, "Online Activism: Media Stereotypes And The Rise Of Smart Mobs," *MasterNewMedia*, June 2007.

13. Kreutz, Christian, "Four examples for innovative mobile phone use in Africa," *CrissCrossed*, August 2007.

14. Belbin, Meredith, *The Coming Shape of Organization*, Butterworth-Heinemann, May 1998.

15. Lipman-Blumen, Jean, and Harold Leavitt, *Hot Groups – Seeding them, feeding them and using them to ignite your organization*, Oxford University Press, 1999.

16. Bennis, Warren, *Organizing Genius – The Secrets of Creative Collaboration*, Nicholas Brealey Publishing, 1997.

17. Moffett, M.. "The Dance of the Electronic Bee," *National Geographic* Volume 77 No. 1 1990.

18. Wilson, Edward and Holldobbler, Bert, *Journey to the Ants*, Harvard University Press, 1994.

19. Brooks, Fred, *The Mythical Man Month*, Addison-Wesley, 1995.

20. Margulis, Lynn, *The Symbiotic Planet – A New Look at Evolution*, Weidenfield & Nicholson, 1998.

21. Meredith, Chris, "The Story of Tit for Tat," *Australian Broadcasting Corporation Online*, 1998.

22. Barabasi, Albert-Laszlo, "Emergence of Scaling in Random Networks," *Science* Volume 286, 1999, pp.509-512.

23. Capra, Fritjoj, *The Web of Life – A New Synthesis of Mind and Matter*, Harper Collins, 1997.

24. Granovetter, Mark, "The strength of weak ties," *American Journal of Sociology*, Issue 6, pp. 1360-1380, 1973.

25. Reynolds, Craig, "Flocks, Herds and Schools – a distributed behaviour mode,l, *Computer Graphics*, pp. 25-34, 1987.

26. Resnick, Mitchel, *Turtles, Termites and Traffic Jams – Explorations in Massively Parallel Microworlds*, MIT Press, 1997.

27. Nowak, Martin, "Why we cooperate," *The Royal Society London*, Webcast (www.royalsoc.ac.uk), 2005.

28. Axelrod, Robert, *The Evolution of Cooperation*, Penguin, 1990.

29. De Geus, Arie, *The Living Company – Growth, Learning and Longevity in Business*, NB Publishing, 1997.

30. Maturana, Humberto and Varela Francisco, *The Tree of Knowledge – The Biological Roots of Human Understanding*, Shambhala 1987.

31. "Are Viruses Alive?" *BeyondBooks.com* www.beyondbooks.com/lif72/2c.asp

32. Capra, Fritjof, *The Hidden Connections*, Flamingo, 2002.

33. Gordon, Deborah, *Ants at Work*, Norton, 1999.

34. Marten, Gerald, *Human Ecology – Basic concepts for sustainable development*, Earthscan, 2003.

35. Kohl , James Vaughn and Francoeur, Robert T, *The Scent of Eros: Mysteries of Odor in Human Sexuality,* iUniverse Inc., 2002.

36. Wyatt, Tristam D, *Pheromones and Animal Behavior – Communication by smell and taste*, Cambridge University Press, 2002.

37. Surowiecki, James, *The Wisdom of Crowds*, Anchor, 2005.

38. Gladwell, Malcolm, *The Tipping Point*, Back Bay Books, 2002.

39. Thompson, Ken, "Teamwork: learning from dolphin pods," *www.bioteams.com*, January 2006

40. Nalebuff, Barry and Adam Brandenburger, *Co-opetition*, Profile Business, September 1997.

41. Anderson, Carl, and Nigel Franks, "Teamwork in animals, robots and humans," *Advances in the Study of Behavior*, pp. 1-27, 1989.

42. Dawkins, Richard, *The Selfish Gene*, Oxford Press, 1989.

43. Duarte, Deborah and Nancy Tennant Snyder, *Mastering Virtual Teams*, Jossey-Bass, 2001.

44. Quick, Tom, "Introduction to Autopoiesis," *University College London*, www.cs.ucl.ac.uk/staff/t.quick/autopoiesis.html

45. Ashby, Ross, *Design for a Brain,* Chapman and Hall, 1960.

46. Espejo, Raul, and Antonia Gill, "The Viable System Model - A briefing about organizational structure," *Synchro Systems*, 2003.

47. Davis. M., *Ecology of Fear - Ecology of fear: Los Angeles and the imagination of disaster*, Metropolitan Books, 1998.

48. Kaplan, Robert and Norton, David, The Balanced Scorecard, *Harvard Business School Press*, 1999.

49. Cross, Rob and Parker, Andrew, The Hidden Power of Social Networks, *Harvard Business School Press*, 2004.

50. Thompson, Ken, "A Taxonomy of Virtual Business Networks", *www.bioteams.com*, July 2005.

51. Keen Andrew, *The Cult of the Amateur: How Today's Internet is Killing Our Culture*, Currency, June 2007.

52.Hof, Robert D, "The Power of Us: Mass Collaboration on The Internet is shaking up Business," *Newsweek Magazine*, June 2005.

53. Mulgan, Geoff, Salem, Omar and Steinberg, Tom, "Wide Open: Open source methods and their future potential," *Demos*, April 2005.

About the Author

Ken Thompson was formerly the European IT Manager with *Reuters* in London, and the Managing Director with VISION Consulting in Belfast. At VISION, Ken spent over 10 years successfully delivering services to clients in the financial services, government and the small business sectors.

Ken is a leading expert in the area of virtual enterprise networks, virtual professional communities and virtual teams. His strategy includes the use of a unique set of team workshops, multiple coaching interventions and the effective integration of a small toolkit of virtual collaboration technologies. He is now developing software, templates and task-specific tools to support the development of high performance teams.

Ken is founder of the www.bioteams.com blog, which is a unique online web site dedicated to the explanation of bioteaming concepts, and to the reporting on new research becoming available in this new study area. The blog is updated regularly and is the definitive source of information on bioteaming.

Meghan-Kiffer Press
Innovation at the Intersection of Business and Technology
Tampa, Florida, USA
www.mkpress.com

New

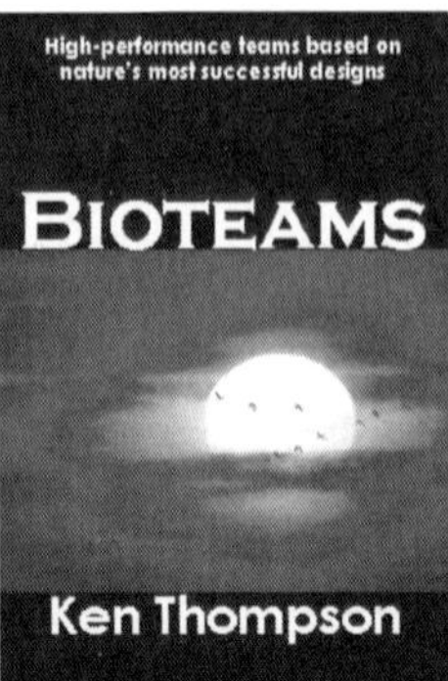

— www.mkpress.com —

Watch:

www.mkpress.com/ShiftHappens